Not too Early, Not Too Late
Life After Retirement

Rev. Dr. James C. Wade, Jr.

Literacy
IN MOTION

Anthony KaDarrell Thigpen Publishers
Indiana

Rev. Dr. James C. Wade, Jr.
Not Too Early– Not Too Late: Life After Retirement

ISBN: 978-0-9904440-1-5
Christians – Religious Life.
Library of Congress Cataloging-in-Publication Data
Printed in the United States of America

Anthony KaDarrell Thigpen, Publisher/Editor-in-Chief
Monice Johnson-Lillie, Co-Editors
Dr. Tyffani Monford-Dent, Co-Editor

For further information contact:
Literacy in Motion Publishing
www.literacyinmotion.com
6212 US Hwy 6, Suite #232
Portage, IN 46368

PO BOX 11892
Merrillville IN 46411
posttribune@hotmail.com
akthigpen@literacyinmotion.com

Not too Early, Not Too Late
James C. Wade, Jr.

*"Those that be planted in the house of the Lord
shall flourish in the courts of our God. They shall
bring forth fruit in old age; they shall be fat and
flourishing; To shew that the Lord is upright: he is
my rock, and there is no unrighteousness in him,"*
(Psalms 92: 13-15).

Content

Acknowledgements

To God belongs the Glory for the privilege of being able to share this book with pastors, churches, and those struggling with retirement. This book is dedicated to my loving wife of 51 years Ella; our children, James III, Camellia, and LaShonta; granddaughter, Brishonda; the-late Dr. J.C. Wade, Sr., my mother, Mary (who prays for everyone); brother and sisters, Rev. Dr. Melvin Wade, Sr., Ruth, and Marsha; my pastor, Rev. Dr. Charles L. Thompson, Jr.; and the Zion Missionary Baptist Church family of East Chicago, Indiana. I would also like to thank Monice Johnson-Lillie and Dr. Tyffani-Monford Dent who shared in the editing of this book; Rev. Dr. Lamont Monford and Rev. Johnny Green for valuable assistance and inspiration; my publisher Anthony KaDarrell Thigpen, and finally, all the pastors who encouraged me to write this book.

Foreword

A Spiritual and Practical Guide to Pastoral Retirement
Monice Johnson-Lillie, Co-Editor

What an honor it is to assist Rev. Dr. J. C. Wade Jr., in such an endeavor as writing this book to assist pastors with transitioning into retirement. Rev. Dr. Wade, Jr. offers a straightforward, spiritual and practical approach to pastoral retirement. In Not Too Early– Not Too Late: Life After Retirement, Rev. Dr. Wade, Jr. utilizes more than 50 years of personal experiences as a pastor, and the wisdom of his deceased father, Rev. Dr. J. C. Wade Sr. who pastored for over four decades. I am humbled by Rev. Dr. Wade, Jr.'s love and concern for pastors struggling with retirement, and the congregations they lead. Although the intent of this book is for pastors, it serves as a useful tool for laypersons as well.

Rev. Dr.Wade, Jr.'s book comes as the result of much prayer and guidance from the Holy Spirit on the Hardship, the How, the Health, and the Hope of transitioning into retirement. Not Too Early– Not

Too Late: Make your Retirement Great is filled with words of wisdom from Rev. Dr. Wade, Jr.'s own experiences, other pastors, preachers, and laypersons, but more importantly it is anchored in the Word of God as he utilizes Biblical scripture references throughout.

Whether you are a young pastor just starting out or one contemplating retirement, Not Too Early– Not Too Late: Life After Retirement is a valuable spiritual and practical tool for planning to transition into a post-pastoral ministry.

Foreword
God Will Bless your Faithfulness
A loving and faithful wife, Mrs. Ella M. Wade

I thank God for how He blessed my husband Rev. Dr. J.C. Wade Jr. during his 50-plus years of pastoral leadership. In the early days of our marriage, there were many occasions where my husband was invited to preach at other churches. No matter the state in which the church was located, the size of the congregation, or whether or not the church was able to provide him accommodations, he recognized the opportunity God was giving him to spread the gospel and did so without hesitation. In his accepting of his Call to Ministry, my husband Rev. Dr. Wade, Jr. was committed to preaching the gospel wherever God led him to do so.

His passion for spreading the Word of God knew no bounds. At his first church, Samaria Baptist Church in Van Alstyne, Texas the congregation was small, but Rev. Dr. Wade Jr. preached as though it was the size of a football stadium. His dedication to the needs of the congregation meant that, at times, we would struggle financially, but my husband never doubted that he was serving God's purpose. There were many weekends Rev. Dr. Wade Jr. would go to the corner store to get $10 worth of groceries using a check, then scramble to the bank on Monday morning to put the funds in to cover it. The owner of the store grew to trust my husband and because of God's blessing he would be at the bank when it opened to cover the check. There was an occasion when Rev. Wade, Jr. preached a two-week revival, commuted every night over 150 miles, and at the end of the two weeks he received $250. Through his ministry, my husband has not only blessed others, but been blessed.

This message goes out to all young pastors; when God blesses you to inherit a harvest you did not plant, don't forget to thank God and always:

- Be Prayerful
- Be Committed
- Be Dedicated
- Be Consistent
- Be Patient
- Be Understanding
- Be Kind to your predecessor
- Be A Proclaimer of the Gospel of Jesus Christ

Be Faithful to God and to the people of God

By following these steps, God will reward you for your faithfulness. Give God every ounce of your Time, your Talent, and your Treasure to do His will His way. I do believe that because of Rev. Dr. Wade Jr.'s faithfulness, God has favored him exceedingly and abundantly above all that he could ask or think.

I am so grateful to God to share these wonderful years with my husband, and to live with a Man of God that loves the Lord, his family, and church. Today, the Lord is blessing him even in retirement to share the Word of God to many all over the world; preaching with the anointing power as well as physical strength that only God can give. Thank you, Lord for this sharing experience of a faithful retired servant of God.

About the Author: Rev. Dr. J.C. Wade, Jr,

Rev. Dr. James Commodore Wade, Jr., a native of Memphis, Tennessee grew up in Omaha, Nebraska and accepted Jesus Christ as his Savior as a child. In 1957, he was licensed as a minister of the gospel and was ordained in 1961 at the Salem Missionary Baptist Church in Omaha, Nebraska. Shortly after his ordination, he was called to pastor Samaria Baptist Church in Van Alstyne, Texas.

After leaving Samaria Baptist Church in 1964, Rev. Dr. Wade, Jr. became pastor of Pilgrim Rest Baptist Church in Van Buren, Arkansas. He remained there until the following year when the Lord called him to take the helm at Zion Missionary Baptist Church in East Chicago, Indiana. Rev. Wade served as pastor for 45 years until his retirement on October 31, 2010. Rev. Dr. Wade, Jr. continues to serve in the position of Pastor Emeritus at Zion Missionary Baptist Church . Rev. Dr. Wade, Jr. also serves as Pastor Emeritus of Greater Destiny Bible Church in East Chicago; a title bestowed upon him by Pastor Kelly Williams.

Rev. Dr. Wade, Jr.'s obtained his Bachelor of Arts Degree, from Bishop College, Dallas, Texas and a Bachelor of Theology from Indiana Christian Bible College in Gary, Indiana. He went on to earn a Master of Religious Education and Doctor of Bible Theology, from International Bible Institute and Seminary in Orlando, Florida. In recognition of his significant contributions to the Christian community, an Honorary Doctor of Divinity was bestowed upon him by GMOR Theological Institute in Gary, Indiana. Rev. Dr. Wade, Jr. has taken his ministry beyond the United States through his extensive studies in Oxford, England as well as making three pilgrimages to the Holy Land where he also preached. Rev. Dr. Wade, Jr. continues to serve as an international evangelist.

Rev. Dr. Wade, Jr. is the former President of the General Missionary Baptist State Convention of Indiana, Inc. and State Vice President of the National Baptist Convention, U.S.A., Inc. His affiliations include the Board of Directors, National Baptist Convention, U.S.A., Division; NAACP; Operation Push; Northwest Indiana Food Bank – implementing an ongoing food pantry; Twin City Ministerial

12

Alliance and Foreign Mission's Preaching Team to Africa.

Rev. Dr. Wade, Jr. is co-author of *These Three*, Volume I, II, and III. During his tenure at Zion Missionary Baptist Church, he oversaw a new church edifice, served as the CEO of the Zion Community Development Corporation, and the After School Tutorial Prevention and Awareness Program Under Rev. Dr. Wade, Jr.'s leadership, in the Zion Academic Academy opened in September 2000, offering early childhood education serves to children ages two to five Rev. Dr. Wade, Jr. has served as devotional leader for the Ministers Seminar of the National Baptist Congress of Christian Education during the tenure of five Presidents of the National Baptist Convention U.S.A., Inc.: Dr. J.H. Jackson, Dr. T.J. Jemison, Dr. Henry S. Lyons, Dr. William J. Shaw, and current President Dr. Julius S. Scruggs.

In May 1994, Rev. Dr. Wade, Jr. was honored with a proclamation from the City of East Chicago, Indiana. In May 2000, the City of East Chicago dedicated and renamed Drummond Street to "Rev. Dr. J.C. Wade,

Jr. Street" for his many years of service and dedication to the community.

Currently, Rev. Dr. Wade, Jr. continues to reside with his wife, Mrs. Ella Wade, in East Chicago, Indiana. They are the proud parents of three children - one son, Rev. James Wade III; two daughters, Camellia McKinley (Pastor Thomas McKinley) and LaShonta Thompson (Pastor Charles Thompson, Jr.) as well as being the grandparents of two granddaughters, Brishonda Wade and Sabrina McKinley; two grandsons, Charles Thompson III and Cameron James Thompson; and one great-grandson, Braylen Chafen.

Rev. Dr. Wade, Jr. is a born-again Christian. He is known as a dynamic preacher and outstanding lecturer throughout the state and across the country. He is an avid community servant who remains diligently committed to the spiritual growth and development for improving the quality of life for youth and families in peril.

A Pastor's Prayer of Confession

The members of the Zion Missionary Baptist Church spoke a prayer of confession over Rev. Dr. Wade, Jr., making daily intercession on his behalf and they continue to do so in his position as Pastor Emeritus. The congregation at Zion understands the importance of scripture, which says, "The prayers of the righteous avails much." These words spoken over Rev. Dr. Wade, Jr. continue to strengthen him even in his post-pastoral ministry.

"I exhort therefore, that, first of all, supplication, prayers, intercessions, and giving of thanks be made for all men; For kings, and for all that are in authority; that we may lead a quiet and peaceful life in all godliness and honesty" (I Timothy. 2: 1-2).

Father, in the name of Jesus, we pray and confess that the Spirit of the Lord shall rest upon Pastor Wade, Jr; the Spirit of Wisdom and Understanding, the Spirit of Counsel and Might, and the Spirit of Knowledge. We pray that as Your Spirit rests upon Pastor Wade, Jr., it will make of him quick understanding because You, Lord have anointed and qualified him to preach the gospel.

You have sent Pastor Wade, Jr. to bind up and heal the broken-hearted, to proclaim liberty to the physical and spiritual captives, and the opening eyes of the prison for those who are bound. Pastor Wade, Jr. shall be called the priest of the Lord; people will speak of him as a minister of God and he shall eat the wealth of the nations and the glory shall be the Lord's.

We pray and believe that no weapon, which is formed against Pastor Wade Jr., shall prosper and that any tongue that rises against him in judgment shall be shown to be in the wrong. We pray that you prosper Pastor Wade, Jr. abundantly, Lord – spiritually, physically, and financially. We confess that Pastor Wade, Jr. holds fast and follows the pattern of wholesome and sound teaching, in all faith and love in Christ Jesus, and that Pastor Wade, Jr. lovingly guards and keeps the truth, which has been entrusted to him by the Holy Spirit.

Lord, we pray that each day freedom and utterance will be given Pastor Wade, Jr.; that he will speak boldly and courageously. Thank you for extra strength that you have given him.

We, thereby confess that we shall stand behind Pastor Wade, Jr. and undergird him in prayer. We will say only those good things, which edify Pastor Wade, Jr. We will not allow ourselves to judge him, but will continue to intercede for him and speak and pray blessings upon him in the name of Jesus. Thank you, Jesus for the answers. Amen."

INTRODUCTION
Divine Purpose in Pastoral Retirement

"Cast me not off in the time of old age; Forsake me not when my strength faileth. Yea, even when I am old and grayheaded, O God, forsake me not, until I have declared thy strength unto the next generation, Thy might to every one that is to come,"
(Psalm 71:9,18).

MY inspiration and motivation for retirement came through my father, Rev. Dr. J.C. Wade, Sr. who served faithfully as pastor of the Salem Baptist Church in Omaha, Nebraska for 44 years. Salem Baptist Church was a small congregation of 99 members when Rev. Dr. Wade, Sr. began pastoring there, and the membership grew in excess of 3,000 before he retired. Salem Baptist Church became an International church and Omaha, Nebraska was placed on the National Convention map.

In December 1997, my father had a heart attack at my sister Ruth Murray's house. While having triple bypass surgery, he suffered a stroke and fell into a coma. The doctor met with my mother Mrs. Mary Wade, my three siblings and me. At that time, we were told that our father would never walk or talk again. It was then that my mother looked the doctor squarely in the eye, telling him, "Doctor, you did all you could do and we're not holding you responsible, but you don't have the last word. I don't mean any harm doctor, but I was not depending on you in the first place. We are going to the chapel and pray and when we leave here from California, my husband will be walking and talking and everybody will know that there is a God in Heaven," When he was released from the hospital, my father and mother, went back to my sister Ruth's house and stayed there for about two weeks before traveling home to Omaha. His road to recovery was not easy. Back in Omaha, my father had to go through physical therapy for a year. Yet, he did the painful work and was well enough to travel back to California and lead a revival for Rev. James Cleveland. After the revival, my father and mother visited with my brother Rev. Melvin Wade, Sr., also a minister, and his wife. While spending the evening in fellowship with my brother and his family, my father again became ill and was taken to the hospital where he remained for six weeks. It was as if we were experiencing an unwanted bout of deja'vu. Afterward when my father was able to travel, my wife and I accompanied him and my mother back to Omaha.

During this time of reoccurring illness, the rigors of physical therapy, and the uncertainty of "what can happen next", my father struggled to balance his need to become physically healthy again, with maintaining the vitality of the church he had led for several decades. After 44 years of preaching, teaching, and leading the Salem Missionary Baptist Church congregation, my father sat down with my brother Melvin and me to share disturbing news. According to my father, a plan was being formed to dismiss him as pastor of the church. Wanting to not cause conflict among his congregants, my father resolved to make the process a smooth one. After much prayer, my father set his retirement date for July 1987. Knowing the responsibilities inherent in pastoral leadership and still possessing a strong love for Salem Missionary Baptist Church, my father also stipulated that, he would not only remain at Salem until another pastor was found, but that he would be fully involved in the selection process and training of the chosen successor. During this planned transition, my father not only established the format for calling the new pastor, but also served as the presiding officer when Rev. Maurice Watson was called to succeed him as pastor. Due to my father's wisdom, foresight, and love for the people he had pastored for so long, Salem Missionary Baptist Church was not without a pastor for a single day.

In looking over my own 45-years as pastor, and reflecting on my father's own admission during his illness that, "Son, I almost stayed too long," my prayer to the Lord was that I didn't serve too long. Yet, I didn't want my own uncertainty to result in my leaving too soon, either. Instead, I wanted to make sure that when I stepped down as pastor, I would be departing on God's timetable. In my interactions with other pastors who have served their congregations for lengthy terms, such a concern about when is "too long" has been an ongoing discussion.

I have listened intently to pastors who have reached maturity tell me how things change and either they have to leave on their own to maintain a sense of dignity, or risk a coupe because they can't "pull it/hoop" like they used to. (You pastors know what I mean...). On the other hand, I have heard and understand the concerns of church members about church attendance decreasing, the overall energy of the church lessening as the pastor's own enthusiasm/energy wanes, and even talking about how they tried to get the pastor to retire, but he refused. As a result, such churches feel compelled to make one of the following decisions: Accept a subpar ministry and let the church continue to go downhill. Ask for the pastor's resignation or dismiss the pastor. In such instances, the members often find themselves forced to choose the same sides that my father assisted his choice in avoiding. The church becomes split in warring factions, ministries become fragmented, and the church loses its mission of being a House of Worship and instead becomes a House of Horrors and Strife.

When called to the ministry and especially to pastor, one takes on the task of serving God and one of his congregations. It is unfair to God and the church for pastors who are no longer able to effectively and energetically serve, to try and "hang on", and I do mean, "hang on." These pastors become stagnant trying to do things they cannot do anymore or are unwilling or unable to lead in a changing/challenging world. Time brings about a change. How tragic it is that so many pastors, who serve faithfully in their ministries, fulfill their mission and vision, but wind up holding on to pastoring long after that has occurred. In doing so, they run the risk of destroying all they have accomplished and wind up leaving with a lot of "exit wounds." Yet, Ecclesiastes 3: 1-2 tells us that *"To everything there is a season, and a time to every purpose under the heaven: A time to be born, and a time to die; a time to plant, and a time to pluck up that which is planted."* It is sad that many of us can quote that scripture, but do not relate it to our own pastoral leadership.

One night some months ago while my wife, granddaughter, and I were preparing to attend a revival I was leading, I was unaware that my 6-year-old great-grandson Braylen would be the one providing a needed lesson. Everyone was dressed and ready to go except Brishonda (who is always running late).

When I said, "Alright let's go, it's that time." Braylen yelled out telling his mother that he was riding with my wife and me whom he referred to as "Gammy"" and "Papa." Braylen's mother asked, "You're not riding with me today?" He quickly replied, "You are not going to waste my time." Of course his mother had a few choice words for him. We left the house with Braylen and arrived at church. After the deacons led devotion, the choir began to sing. Braylen had a strange look on his face. My wife asked him what was wrong and he responded, "Those people are too old, and it's only a few of them. So, "Gammy", I'm going to sleep." Several weeks after the revival, Braylen went back to the same church with his mother. As they drove up to the church, Braylen stared in disbelief. Disappointed, he stated, "Mama we're back here again."

At such a young age, Braylen was uttering the sentiments of youth who go to churches where the pastor and the majority of people within the congregation have grown old and there are very few young people. When the majority of a church's congregation is filled with senior citizens, the energy level is low and the atmosphere becomes dull and dry. As a result, younger Christians lose interest and drift away from the church.

Pastors are like athletes. Early on, they possess the energy, and new knowledge that can make them exceptional with the right coaching. They may be the most skilled in the middle of their pastoral life because they have increased their knowledge and abilities while being able to continue to learn from those around them. The energy level is still high and often remains focused on the vision and mission of the church. However, there is also that more seasoned pastor; the one who can no longer compete at a certain level, but is always looking for a comeback. He believes that he "still has more in him, even though his health, energy, interest, or enthusiasm continues to wane. This pastor is the one who does not recognize or refuses to acknowledge that it's gone and never to return, but thank God for what He's already done in our life and ministry." This pastor is the one who may struggle to see that he can continue to serve God, but not in the pulpit.

The decision to retire can be a difficult one, and there are important concerns that need to be addressed for pastors contemplating or planning this transition. Such concerns often generate questions such as: How does a pastor know when it is time to retire? What should a pastor desire to do once he/she retires? What should a pastor focus on (purpose) once retired? To what extent does productivity and persistence play in the life of a retired pastor? Finally, in seeking God's will, is this retirement the result of Divine Providence? Jeremiah 33:3 says, *"Call unto me, and I will answer thee, and shew thee great and mighty things, which thou knowest not."*

As it relates to the productivity and persistence of retirement, one must have a second ministry after the pastoral ministry ends. Proverbs 29: 18 warns us, *"Where there is no vision, the people perish: but he that keepeth the law, happy is he."* Habakkuk 2: 1-4 states: *"I will stand upon my watch, and set me upon the tower, and will watch to see what he will say unto me, and what I shall answer when I am reproved. And the LORD answered me, and said, Write the vision, and make it plain upon tables, that he may run that readeth it. For the vision is yet for an appointed time, but at the end it shall speak, and not lie: though it tarry, wait for it; because it will surely come, it will not tarry. Behold, his soul which is lifted up is not upright in him: but the just shall live by his faith."* Throughout this book, I will address in more detail the concerns associated with transitioning from serving as pastor, as well as the challenges and needs in doing so decently and in order.

When I left home in 1957 to attend Bishop College, I preached only my third sermon as a young preacher in the ministers-lyceum. At that time, I was severely criticized and even heard comments made by some of the upper classmen who huddled together and (falsely, I like to think) predicted, "Poor Wade will never make it as a preacher." Unbeknownst to them, I overheard their statement, went back to my dorm room, and fell prostrate on the floor seeking

God's affirmation. I needed to know I am called by God to preach the gospel. That same night God gave me confirmation when He spoke into my spirit saying, "I called and anointed you to be a prophet to the Nations."

In spite of doubts from my fellow ministers about my commitment and ability to gain the skills needed to preach, I knew that it was God's faith in my ability that was important. I not only threw myself into my biblical studies, but I became an active part of student life by being the lead tenor soloist in the Bishop College Choir and touring across the country. I knew that my education as a minister and pastor were just beginning as I was called and accepted the call to pastor Samaria Baptist Church in Van Alstyne, Texas. Yet, even my road to Samaria Baptist was my first inkling of how a blueprint for pastoral transition was needed and could manifest itself. I graduated from Bishop College with my Bachelor of Arts Degree in the summer of 1961.

During the fall season, when I was called to pastor Samaria Baptist Church, I had to think about my own growth as a minister/orator. Reflecting back on how the upperclassmen had wrongly predicted my inability to pastor, it was an actual pastor, Rev. G.A.

Hobart Shepherd who had recognized my ability to do so. After preaching at New Friendship Baptist Church in Dallas, Texas, Rev. Shepherd, who was also visiting at the time, asked me if I wanted to become a pastor. Without hesitation, I responded with an emphatic "Yes!" He then told me about Samaria Baptist Church in Van Alstyne. The following day after talking with Rev.

Reflecting back on how the upperclassmen had wrongly predicted my inability to pastor...

Shepherd, I saw a pastor named Rev. Vernie Perry and asked him about Samaria Baptist Church. To my surprise, he informed me, "Boy, I used to pastor that church." Rev. Perry offered to take me to Van Alstyne and introduce me to the Chairman of the Deacon Board. This initial connection and support of Rev. Perry contributed to the Chairman, Bro. Hugh Orr inviting me to preach a three-night revival at Samaria. Shortly after that I began serving as its pastor, a position I would hold until early 1964.

After a year of pastoring at Samaria I married Ella Hodge. I had only been married to my wife for three months. Nine months later God blessed us with a son. I was beginning the process many new pastors experience of having to balance pastoral duties, a young marriage, and what was then an infant son. During those days, we also dealt with the reality of sometimes-difficult financial situations around serving as a pastor. It was pretty rough on my family because I was making only about $11.75 some Sundays, with a good day earning $25. I prayed to God one night that I needed financial deliverance because we were struggling pretty badly. Within three months, God allowed me to receive a call from Pilgrim Rest Church in Van Buren, Arkansas where I served as pastor for about seven months until February 1965, when I began serving as pastor of the Zion Missionary Baptist Church in East Chicago, Indiana, where I would remain until my retirement in October, 2010.

While pastoring at Samaria Baptist Church, I remember driving the 1953 Ford given to me by the church because I had to commute between Dallas and Van Alstyne. One day when I went to start the car, it began to shake. It seemed as if the motor was going to fly out of the car. After taking it to the service station, the mechanic raised the hood, took a screwdriver and made some adjustments to the carburetor. Afterward, the car settled down and I drove off. As pastors, we are no different than that 1953 Ford. As we get older, and make the transition from being pastors to retiring pastors, all we have to do is what that mechanic did with that screwdriver; make a little adjustment and life will settle down and run more smoothly. **"You can go on!"** I kept that 1953 Ford so long that one day when I went out to get in the car, the motor was sitting on the ground and I had to have it hauled away because I had kept it too long. Sometimes as pastors, we stay too long and the people have to make decisions on whether to continue to keep us or have us hauled away. Many times we stay too long and our ministry loses its usefulness. It literally drags the ground and the motor runs out; rendering it lifeless. On the other hand, by making preparation for transitioning, we can leave with dignity. It's bad to stay over your time, and it's not good to leave before time. A perfect example of not letting new opportunities keep one from fulfilling God's responsibilities is the offer I received from New Zion Baptist Church.

In 1977, while pastoring Zion Missionary Baptist Church in East Chicago, Indiana, I was called to pastor the New Zion Baptist Church in New

Orleans, Louisiana. At that time we were in a new building program at Zion Missionary Baptist Church. I accepted the call to pastor New Zion, and as a result I commuted back and forth for three months; dividing my time between New Zion in New Orleans, and Zion M.B, Church in East Chicago. In order to assist Zion Missionary Baptist Church find a new pastor, I used the traditional method and appointed a Pulpit Committee instructing them to go in prayer and allow the Holy Spirit to give them another pastor. However, in the mist of commuting between both churches, I witnessed some things at Zion Missionary Baptist Church, which took me back to when my father was ill and his church was going through transition. I began seeing an atmosphere of power struggle; constantly being asked the question, "Who is going to run it (the church)?" There were power plays among the membership, and a struggle over the mantle. When I saw this, I knew that I did not ever want Zion Missionary Baptist Church to go through that season again. That moment of deja'vu caused me to pray, "Lord, I don't ever want Zion Missionary Baptist Church to be without a pastor." It was then that the Holy Spirit said, "No, go home," and Zion Missionary Baptist Church in East Chicago was home. My fervent prayer was that I would retire one Sunday from Zion M.B Church and the very next Sunday, a new pastor would take the helm. God granted my prayers, and I remained at Zion Missionary Baptist Church until I retired from pastoring.

Yet, there was nothing in place for transitioning. I used the old traditional method of appointing a pulpit committee, and I watched the church go through a spirit of division that I had never witnessed. In my period of devotion, I discovered it was never God's design that laymen pastor churches. He even tells us in Jeremiah 3:15: *"And I will give you pastors according to mine heart, which shall feed you with knowledge and understanding."* God further cautions us on not allowing those who are not attempting to do what is best for His church to make decisions about its leadership or direction. In Acts 20: 28-30, God warns us. *"Take heed therefore unto yourselves, and to all the flock, over that which the Holy Ghost hath made you overseers, to feed the church of God, which he hath purchased with his own blood. (29) For I know this, that after my departing shall grievous wolves enter in among you, not sparing the flock. (30) Also of y our own selves shall men arise, speaking perverse things, to draw away disciples after them."* After reading these scriptures, I prayed that God would give me guidance through the power and ministry of the Holy Spirit that our church would never be without a pastor, not even for one day.

I remained at Zion Missionary Baptist Church for 45 years and approximately five years before my retirement I began to share that prayer with our church leaders. Many did not want to discuss the possibility of my retirement or the need for a transition process, but the Holy Spirit would not let me divorce myself from it. Instead, I not only shared my prayer and God's wishes with the leadership of the church, but also began speaking about it from the pulpit. God kept this in my spirit and I was determined to keep it alive in the church.

In my discussion of this with the church's leadership and with the congregation as a whole, I began reflecting on my father's experience, that of other pastors I knew, my own observations, and scripture. In this learning process, I had to begin to answer the question: When does a pastor know it is time to transition into retirement? There is a simple, yet very powerful answer to that question. You know that it is time to retire when you pray, pray, and pray some more because when God calls you He sends you forth. God gives us clear direction of the power in our prayers as it relates to guidance about our next steps. Matthew 7: 7-8, *"Ask, and it shall be given you; seek, and ye shall find; knock, and it shall be opened unto you: (8)For every one that asketh receiveth; and he that seeketh findeth; and to him that knocketh it shall be opened."* St. John 14: 13-14, *"And whatsoever ye shall ask in my name, that will I do, that the Father may be glorified in the Son. (14) If ye shall ask any thing in my name, I will do it."*

When we pray God hears. God will answer, God will intervene, God will come, God will show up, and when He shows up, He will show out. Grandma always said, "He's an on time God, yes He is." One songwriter wrote:

> *"You can't hurry God,*
> *O' no you just have to wait.*
> *You have to trust Him and give Him time,*
> *No matter how long it takes.*
> *He's a God, you can't hurry,*
> *He'll be there don't you worry.*
> *He may not come when you want Him,*

But He's right on time"

In his book It Happens After Prayer: Biblical Motivation for Believing Prayer, Rev. H.B. Charles of the Shiloh Metropolitan Baptist Church in Jacksonville, Florida said, "Prayer is a privilege. It is not a burdensome duty. It is a wonderful privilege. Even though scripture commands us to pray, we should not view prayer as something we have to do. We should view it as something we get to do. It is a privilege to have an audience before the Creator and Sustainer of the universe. Prayer works! More accurately, God works when we pray. When we

work, we work. When we pray, God works." Charles Spurgeon, a British Baptist preacher born in 1834 said, "Prayer is the nerve that moves the arm of the Omnipotent." Prayer is not vain speculation; instead it is one of the most powerful tools we have within our arsenal. My grandmother had a favorite song that emphasized the power of prayer:

"What a friend we have in Jesus, all our sins and griefs to bear!
What a privilege to carry, everything to God in prayer!
O, what peace we often forfeit, O, what needless pain we bear,

All because we do not carry, everything to God in prayer!

Have we trials and temptations? Is there trouble anywhere?
We should never be discouraged, take it to the Lord in prayer.
Can we find a friend so faithful, who will all our sorrows share?
Jesus knows our every weakness, take it to the Lord in prayer.

Are we weak and heavy-laden, cumbered with a load of care:
Precious Savior, still our refuge, take it to the Lord in prayer.
Do thy friends despite, for sake thee? Take it to the Lord in prayer;
In His arms He'll take and shield thee: Thou wilt find a solace there."

When it is time for transitioning, the same God who called you to your present pastoral ministry will also reassign you to a post-pastoral ministry. When we realize as pastors that it is not about us and it is all about God, we will re-evaluate our post-pastoral ministry. This book focuses on four areas that are essential to a pastor's understanding of transitioning into retirement.

- The *Hardship* of Transition
- The *How* of Transition
- The *Hope* of Transition
- The *Health* of Transition

After reading <u>Not Too Early– Not Too Late: Life After Retirement</u>, it is my prayer that pastors, as well as laypersons have a spiritual and practical understanding of *why* retirement is necessary, *when* it needs to take place, and *how* one needs to plan for it.

This book focuses on four areas that are essential to a pastor's understanding of transitioning into retirement.

- The *Hardship* of Transition
- The *How* of Transition
- The *Hope* of Transition
- The *Health* of Transition

The "Hardship" of Transition

"Fear thou not; I am with thee:
be not dismayed; for I am thy God:
I will strengthen thee; yea, I will help
thee; yea, I will uphold thee with
the right hand of my righteousness"
(Isaiah 41: 10).

Our time waiting on when we transition from pastoring should not involve complacency. We are still commissioned to do God's work. We must claim the territory for God's righteousness. Your present assignment must be a long-time commitment. You must become enthusiastic about the place where you serve. Sometimes, we are not clear as to why God has chosen us to lead a certain church, especially when conflict is occurring. However, we must remember that God puts us in place for a reason. What God has done assures us of what He will continue to do. Psalms 40: 1 reminds us (To the chief Musician, a Psalm of David) *"I waited patiently for the Lord: and he inclined unto me, and heard my cry."* What an awesome God who never sleeps nor slumbers, and comes and sees about us! Psalm 40:5 tells us: *"Many, O Lord my God, are thy wonderful works which thou hast done, and thy thoughts which are to us-ward: they cannot be reckoned up in order unto thee: if I would declare and speak of them, they are more than can be numbered."* The Lord has performed many miracles and His plans for us are too numerous to list. A.W. Tozer , author of The Pursuit of God said, "God is looking for people through whom He can do the impossible. What a pity that we plan only the things that we can do ourselves." In pastoring, we must not get to the point where we believe that we are solely responsible for the success of our ministry. When we "begin to believe the hype", we leave ourselves vulnerable to making major mistakes and becoming consumed with the possibility of failure. Yet, when we remember that God leads us and His Church, Psalm 34: 4 gives us the message that: *"I sought the Lord, and he heard me, and delivered me from all my fears."* I prayed to the Lord, and He answered me, freeing me from all my fears. When we trust God by faith, God will give inner peace, regardless of our circumstances. He will then permit us to do what Psalm 3:5 states: *"I laid me down and slept; I awaked; for the Lord sustained me."* Leaning on God allows us to know that, *though a mighty army surrounds me, my heart will know no fear; even if they attack me I remain confident.* We can have assurance in God's promise because God is truth. He cannot and does not lie. Hebrew 6:18 asserts *"That by two immutable things, in which it was impossible for God to lie, we might have a strong consolation, who have fled to refuge to lay hold upon the hope set before us"* God has promised to bless his people. God will bless you when you remember that God promises to bring a harvest of blessings in his perfect time. Galatians 6:9 assures us *"And let us not be weary in well doing: for in due season we shall reap; if we not faint."* Don't get tired of doing what is good. Don't be discouraged and give up, for we will reap a harvest of blessing at the appropriate time. In every circumstance, God cares.

There is a great harvest to be had in the world. God always calls us to do something greater than ourselves; something bigger than we can accomplish on our own. That's because He wants us to rely on Him. Don't let yourself become distracted from what He has called you to do. Stay focused on Him who called you, and He is the Lord God. There is no right way to do wrong and there is no wrong way to do right. Do the right thing because the right thing is the thing to do. The Lord does not go out of business when churches go out of business. A church goes out of business because it has uncommitted Christians who choose to no longer do the Lord's work. .

In his book, *The Purpose Driven Life*, Rick Warren said, "You were planned for God's pleasure." The best way to live is to surrender to Jesus Christ. Surrender is not the best way to live; it is the only way to live. Nothing else works. All other approaches lead to frustration, disappointment, and self-destruction. The King James Version calls surrender "your reasonable service." Another version translates it as "the most sensible way to serve God." Sometimes it takes years, but eventually we discover that the greatest hindrance to God's blessing in our life is not others, but it is ourselves – our own self-will, stubborn pride, and personal ambition.

You cannot fulfill God's purpose for your life while focusing on your own plans. If God is going to do his deepest work in you, it must begin with His will, His work, and His way. I remember during my early days of pastoring when my wife and I were struggling financially. I received a call one day to work a job where I would make some pretty good money; a lot more than I was making as a pastor. My wife and I were so excited. However, when I met with the manager, he told me I would have to work on Sundays. Well, I told him that I needed to be off on Sundays because I was the pastor of a church. The manager told me that if I was not able to work on Sundays he would have to find someone else for the position. Well, I went home and told my wife that I would not be taking the job because it would require me to work on Sundays. Although obviously disappointed, my wife's support for me never faltered. It was not God's will for me to take that job. Give it all to God - your past regrets, your present problems, your future ambition, your fears, dreams, weaknesses, habits, hurts, and hang-ups. Put Jesus Christ first in your life. Don't be afraid. Nothing under His control can ever be out of control. Mastered by Christ, you can handle anything. You will be like Paul when he said, *"I am ready for anything and equal to anything through Him who infuses inner strength into me, that is, I am self-sufficient in Christ's sufficiency."* Dr. Joel Gregory, Professor of Preaching at the George W. Truett Theological Seminary at Baylor University said, "Life has opportunities and we must seize them and not merely play safe." Just because life is uncertain, does not mean we should do nothing. We must demonstrate a spirit of trust and adventure, facing life's risks and opportunities with direct enthusiasm and faith in God. The actions of God are beyond human calculation. Hebrews 11: 1, 2 and 6 reminds us *(1) "Now faith is the substance of things hoped for, the evidence of things not seen" (2) "For by it the elders obtained a good report." (6) "But without faith it is impossible to please him: for he that cometh to God must believe that he is, and that he is a rewarder of them that diligently seek him."*

Pastors are human. At times, we doubt not only our message, but the plan God has for our ministry and our life." <u>Revitalize</u> the value of life even with its uncertainties. We must trust God for the <u>unknown and the unknowable</u>. Just because one cannot know the work of God does not make it any less true. God has made everything appropriate to go ahead and act. In other words, because God is who He is and what He has done, it's alright to go ahead and give up the luxury of being certain. Sometimes, many things we do for God do not make sense to us. We may even see them as absurd. This is called the absurdity view. To some it seems senseless, but trusting God by faith is by no means absurd or senseless. When we trust God by faith, there will be a return of divine blessings. When we trust God by faith, we know that the laws of nature will be faithful in their course. In Ecclesiastes 11:1-6: *we are told (1) "Cast thy bread upon the waters: for thou shalt find it after many days." (2) "Give a portion to seven, and also to eight; for thou knowest not what evil shall be upon the earth." (3) "If the clouds be full of rain, they empty themselves upon the earth: and if the tree fall* toward the south, or toward the north, in the place where the tree falleth, there it shall be." (4) "He that observeth the wind shall not sow; and he that regardeth the clouds shall not reap." (5) "As thou knowest not what is the way of the spirit, nor how the bones do grow in the womb of her that is with child: even so thou knowest not the works of God who maketh all." (6) "In the morning sow thy seed, and in the evening withhold not thine hand: for thou knowest not whether shall prosper, either this or that, or whether they both shall be alike good." When you cast your bread upon the water it will return. When clouds are full of rain and it becomes heavy, they will empty themselves upon the earth. When you cut a tree down it will fall to the earth. When you sow seed it will bring forth increase.

For many years I heard my father say, "If you cast your bread upon the water it will come back with butter on it." He added an addendum to that and said, "When you cast your bread upon the water God will send it back with butter and jelly on it." As my father told me, bread does not sink. I have discovered in my life that when you share with others, the good that you give will come back to you. During my days as pastor of Zion Missionary Baptist Church, I shared with pastors, ministers, associate ministers, and laypersons. The good I shared with them now comes back to me, and also to my wife. We are being used for special occasions, seminars, workshops, children ministries, and many other areas of ministry. So, pastors while in your hay-days cast your bread upon the water; so, in your declining days God will send back blessings where you won't have room enough to receive.

When you give you know that you will gain. What is given will not dissipate or vanish. You must be willing to lose in order to gain what God has for you. The sacrifices you make when trying to do God's work is not in vain. Giving will not get lost. Whatever I have imparted I will possess. St. Luke 6: 38 reinforces this by reminding us *"Give, and it shall be given unto you; good measure, pressed down, and shaken together, and running over, shall men give into your bosom. For with the same measure that ye mete withal it shall be measured to you again."*

In an excerpt from *Raising a Brand New Bar* motivational speaker Michael Applegate says, "Nothing just happens!" Psalm 37:23 seems to also support this by stating, *"The steps of a good man are ordered by the Lord and he delighteth in his way."* God has positioned us so that we can be motivators and representatives for His divine purpose. When you are a motivator then it is your assignment, your responsibility and your mission to motivate others. We are responsible to raise a higher standard. We should not just do anything halfway. Phil Jackson, former Head Coach of the Chicago Bulls and the Los Angeles Lakers once said, "You win from within." Thank God for this statement of fact because when you retire, you have to do it from "within." God through the Holy Spirit must confirm in your heart that you have to be content from within. We must not be envious or jealous of younger preachers and pastors. These younger preacher and pastor will give renewed life and energy to the church. It takes energy to pastor a church. Let's be for real, as we get older we just don't have it like we use to.

As I began to look seriously at retirement, I saw signs that moved me to my decision to retire from pastoring, but not from preaching. Times change, and I saw the world move from the position of "Me" to that of "I"---, I-Zooms, I-Phones, I-Pods, I-Tunes, I-Max, and so on. Just as technology was advancing quickly, this season of change also happened somewhat suddenly. Personally, I just could not keep up with all of the technological advances that were becoming the norm within pastoral leadership, even though I had a staff that could. It was during this season of rapid technological innovation that I began to see the church moving in this high-tech direction, and leaving me behind. Like any person who grew up in my generation, technological know-how was not something I had learned at birth. I watched as those younger than me navigated what was so foreign. Although I did have an efficient staff who kept me abreast of things, I still felt out of my element and floundering in a sea of laptops, social networking, and smart phones. Even more troubling was my having to admit that I had no desire to learn because I had become stagnant and satisfied with what I knew. Even in this admission, I understood that what I knew and what I needed to know to be an effective pastor were two very different things.

For those who are in the Post-Pastoral Age (that age when you know that you can't keep up with the changing times) there will be signs that it's time to retire. For example, my church has an early morning worship service at 7:30 a.m., Sunday School at 9:00 a.m., morning worship service at 10:30 a.m., and evening worship service at 6:00 p.m. When I realized that I was unable to give my best to each and every service, I knew it was time to retire. When I could miss teaching Bible Study and not feel bad, I knew it was time to retire. When I would come home from church on Sunday after a full day and it took me two days to physically and emotionally recover, I knew it was time for me to retire. Many pastors reach a certain age of maturity and have what the old folks called the "make do, anything will do" syndrome. This "pastoral ailment" involves just doing enough to get by. If you know you don't have "it" anymore, but you continue to hang on and hang around, you lose your effectiveness and eventually your credibility.

As a pastor, when you can't give God your best at *all* times, it's time to retire. Like technology passing you by, this is another sign that it is time for your Post-Pastoral Ministry to begin. When you have to send someone else because you either cannot go or you don't have the desire to go yourself, it is time for your Post-Pastoral Ministry. When you see things in ministry not at their full potential and instead of addressing the issue, you remain quiet hoping and praying that it will just get better knowing it will not without your active intervention----it is time for your

Post-Pastoral Ministry. When you see your energy level waning, and you lose most of your stamina, **it's time!** When thinking and reflexes are not as sharp as they used to be and you see the negative effect it has on the church's progress, **it's time!** When your mind says you can, but your body says you cannot, **it's time!** Failure to move forward to Post-Pastoral Ministry when the signs are there to do so, results in your being "in the way" instead of "helping to make a way." You become a fixture that no longer serves its purpose, and not a fix-it. The Bible says in II Timothy 4:5 (latter part), *"Make full proof of your ministry."* The Revised Standard Version says, *"Fulfill your ministry."* The New Revised Standard Version says, *"Carry out your ministry fully."* Leave nothing undone that you ought to do. The New International Version says, *"Discharge all the duties of your ministry."* Some could argue that I was doing what the Bible orders because people were still coming to church. They were still in the balcony on Sunday mornings. Yet, that alone is not a sign of a healthy church. People may love being in the crowd, but is your ministry blessing them? Sometimes, it is not your pastoral leadership that remains fresh, but something else within the church that draws people in and sustains it. Yet, no matter how wonderful the choir, how exciting the praise dance team, if your pastoral leadership is not providing guidance and understanding of God's word, the church becomes a place of entertainment and not a Place of Worship. At our church, we had the Zion Missionary Baptist Church Academy (ZMBC), which was known nationally as a top-rated academy. This academy drew many to the church. Yet, when my daughter Camillia McKinley, who served as the Director relocated, the academy closed and I had neither the energy nor the life to help keep it alive. Again, it was not my pastoral leadership that was maintaining the church, as it should, and when I was put to the test to pour my energy in to that successful ministry, I could not. I knew **it was time!**

Energy is not limited to sustaining a program, but also to bringing fresh perspectives in the teaching part of the ministry. I have been a serious preacher-pastor for years, a true student of the Word. Conducting Bible Class was one of my favorite things to do on Wednesday at 12:00 noon and 6:00 p.m. It had blessed our church and me. However, when I found myself going back to some of the old lessons and sermons that I taught or preached over the years, instead of immersing myself in to the scripture to make Bible lessons relevant to a newer generation and new life circumstances, the church became a preaching station rather than a witnessing, redeeming community. When this occurs, it is time for you to move on or risk the church moving you on.

At times, one of the reasons it is so hard to transition into retirement is **pride**. The middle letter in "Pride" is "I." The middle letter in "Sin" is "I." What turns the word "Run" into "Ruin" is "I." When "I" try to "Run it past God's time", "I Ruin it." Pride tightens the grip on leadership. It will always hinder the move of God in your life, and sometimes it can be present and you don't even know it. It is surprising how many pastors and the spirit of pride adversely affects people in the body of Christ. It blinds you to truth, if it is left unchecked. Pride can bring you low. Proverbs 29:23 tells us *"A man's pride shall bring him low; but honour shall uphold the humble in spirit,"* Proverbs 29:2 says, *"When the righteous are in authority, the people rejoice: but when the wicked beareth rule, the people mourn."* Let God have his way in your life. Pride can get in the way of pastoral leadership as Proverb 16:18 cautions us: *"Pride goeth before destruction, and an haughty spirit before a fall,"*

Other translations say, *"First pride, then the crash. The bigger the ego, the harder the fall." "Pride is the first step to destruction. Proud thoughts will lead you to defeat."*

The church belongs to God. Sometimes, we as pastors forget this. We begin to believe that the church exists solely because of our leadership. In this belief, we resist stepping down and continue believing that God will take care of His church. It is sad that so many pastors stay until the church goes down and then the next pastor has to struggle for several years trying to get it back up. Sometimes, the new pastor is even put in the unenviable position of having to take the mantle out of some of the leaders' hands. I call this "transferred authority," which is certainly not pastoral authority. Instead, it is laymen authority, which is not biblical. Yet, when we as pastors fail to utilize our pastoral authority by recognizing that the church belongs to God and we should only lead it as long as we are truly able; and by not acknowledging and therefore not planning for what the church will do when we retire from pastoral leadership, we damage the church. In his book <u>The Top Ten Mistakes Leaders Make</u>, Hans Finzel advises, "Plan your departure the day you begin." Darryle L. Brister in his book Against All Odds reminds us, "If you cannot see beyond the immediate, you will have no reason to prepare for the future."

My brother, Rev. Dr. Melvin Wade, Sr., Senior Pastor at Mt. Moriah Baptist Church in Los Angeles, California says, "In this day and time, there is much discussion about whether or not a pastor should retire from pastoring. I have witnessed across the years, those who did and those who did not. I am thoroughly convinced that stepping aside before it is too late is the better choice. I am convinced that my brother James (Rev. Dr. Wade, Jr.), after much consultation with God, is a classic example of one who stepped aside before it was too late. The initiative to step aside was not a rash decision and was based on Proverb 3:4-6, "*So shalt thou find favour and good understanding in the sight of God and man. (5)Trust in the LORD with all thine heart; and lean not unto thine own understanding. (6)In all thy ways acknowledge him, and he shall direct thy paths.*" He trusted God and recognized that for God's church to continue to thrive, he must turn over pastoral leadership before it was too late. Yet, in being open to God's plan for his life and for his post-pastoral ministry, God has kept him (Rev. Dr. Wade, Jr.) proclaiming the unsearchable riches of Christ. He has embraced that ministry does not end when one follows God's wishes to turn over the pastoral role, and has accepted his new assignment to counsel and mentor young pastors. I take this moment to commend my brother, my best friend, for not only stepping down from pastoral ministry before it was too late, but for also stepping aside with a plan to remain active in the ministry."

In his ability to step aside and acknowledge that one is not as effective as he once was, one notes that the church is bigger than him. This is a perfect example of the principle that makes transitioning easier – humility. Humility relaxes and lets go. Letting go of leadership is like sending your children away to college; it might hurt, but it has to be done. The Reaching through Teaching Ministries in their lesson on Biblical Succession in Training Successors reminds us "the Lord does not give us a responsibility in the kingdom to exalt and/or lift us up. God expects us to humbly serve His people. He also expects us to relinquish our responsibility to another in His timing. Psalms 75:6-7 teaches us, *"For promotion cometh neither from the east, nor from the west, nor from the south. But God is the judge: he putteth down one, and setteth up another."*

We see people struggling to pass the mantle on in all walks of life. Since the law changed banning most employers from being able to force their employees to retire, the workforce has aged significantly. This is not necessarily a bad thing as older workers often means a wealth of experience; however, we need to be honest with ourselves and willing to pass the mantle on when we can no longer perform at the capacity needed for the position. The Reaching through Teaching Ministries' lesson on Biblical Succession in Training Successors also states "one secret to successful leadership is to hold positions lightly. The harder we hang on to a position, the more difficult it becomes to release it at the appropriate time."

Considered one of the most influential American church leaders of the last 100 years, Lyle Schaller said, "Of all the leadership transition mistakes, two occur most frequently. Pastors tend to stay too long in a position and develop a declining and graying congregation. There are other pastors not staying long enough." Pastors who stay too long do much more damage than those who don't stay long enough. In choosing to stay too long, pastors do not acknowledge that someone else needs to take their place. When we neglect to recognize this it leads to no planning for a successor. Success without a successor is failure. The question that must be answered is, who are you grooming to one day take your place? The pastor is to serve God and the church. One must remember that the church will live or die based upon the flow of new leadership in the church.

There were two pastors who had previously been Wide Receivers on their respective professional football teams. They were discussing the fact that both of them carried in plays to the quarterback for the next play. As they were discussing their football exploits, one said to the other, "if we could ever get our churches to receive the plays from the Holy Spirit, the coach of the church; whom he gets from Jesus, the offensive coordinator; who calls the plays that he gets from God the owner, who designed the playbook which is the Bible; and the people receive the plays through the pastor; how wonderful would that be. This provides the understanding that the plays from our biblical playbook are passed to our pastor (the earthen vessel) who hands it off to the congregation.

Just like those two pastors who were professional football players had likely started out playing for their high school or college teams, young ministers who are in the position to inherit great ministries must be patient enough to let God direct their calling. Being called a pastor is not what makes you a pastor. Just like Paul instructed and mentored Timothy in the ministry, younger pastors need the same kind of guidance and teaching from more seasoned pastors.

A few days ago I was watching a program on the NATGEO Network. The show followed a group of lions known as a "pride." A number of new cubs had been born to the pride. One day, two young nomadic male lions came to take over the pride. In order to do so, they had to defeat the head male member of the pride. Being young, these nomadic male lions appeared to believe that overthrowing the older males would be easy, as they possessed superior strength. These young, naïve, and inexperienced nomadic males came in, but what they did not know was that females fight to the death to protect their young. Instead of the older and already established pride male having to defend the group, the females went on the attack and ran the two young male lions off. These nomadic males did not know the traditions/rules of the pride. They were unfamiliar with the pride culture, instead putting too much emphasis on the superficial characteristic of physical strength. In coming in to pastoral leadership when another pastor has transitioned or is transitioning, young pastors must learn from the mistakes of the nomadic lions.

Young pastors, be careful that you don't make the mistake of moving too soon when you go into a new situation and the pastor has been there for a number of years. You must learn the culture of the church that you are leading. You must be open to acknowledging the value in some of its traditions while still bringing your own strength (knowledge/energy/creativity) to it. Not valuing the church that existed before you walked in to its doors could result in you being faced with resistance and rebellion from the congregation. They may call you pastor, but you have to become their pastor through your actions. One wins favor with the people of God when you earn their respect. When you take time out to visit the sick, bury the dead, and comfort those that are mourning. When the members of the church see you loving God, and loving the people of God, they will gladly give you the mantle and allow you to serve them.

The two young male lions came with the mindset that they needed to fight for leadership, but you don't have to fight for it. You don't have to fuss for it and you don't have to engage in power struggles. When you wait on God, He will give you the fulfillment of His promise, which is found in Jeremiah 3:15: *"And I will give you pastors according to mine heart, which shall feed you with knowledge and understanding."*

Young pastors and preachers must learn the value in patience and waiting. Going back to the nomadic lions, if they would have waited until the lionesses had weaned their young, they would not have had to battle them. Instead, they would have only to contend with the older males in the pride. Timing is very important; as a matter of fact, it is crucial and critical to your pastoral development. LEARN TO WAIT. Waiting does not mean doing nothing; waiting means moving by the unction of the Holy Spirit. St. John 14: 23-27 reminds us: *"Jesus answered and said unto him, If a man love me, he will keep my words: and my Father will love him, and we will come unto him, and make our abode with him." (24) "He that loveth me not keepeth not my sayings: and the word which ye hear is not mine, but the Father's which sent me."(25) "These things have I spoken unto you, being yet present with you." (26) "But the Comforter, which is the Holy Ghost, whom the Father will send in my name, he shall teach you all things, and bring all things to your remembrance, whatsoever I have said unto you." (27) "Peace I leave with you, my peace I give unto you: not as the world giveth, give I unto you. Let not your heart be troubled, neither let it be afraid."*

In 45-plus years as pastor, there were times when I wanted to do things on my own schedule, but I had to wait. When you don't wait on God, you tend to make a mess of things. It is then when you think back and wish you had waited. God's time is not our time, and in waiting He will strengthen us. Isaiah 40: 28-31asks us: *"Hast thou not known? hast thou not heard, that the everlasting God, the LORD, the Creator of the ends of the earth, fainteth not, neither is weary? there is no searching of his understanding." (29) "He giveth power to the faint; and to them that have no might he increaseth strength." (30) "Even the youths shall faint and be weary, and the young men shall utterly fall:" (31), "But they that wait upon the* LORD *shall renew their strength; they shall mount up with wings as eagles; they shall run, and not be weary; and they shall walk, and not faint."*

Again, being on God's timetable is two-fold: being patient as it relates to assuming leadership through a transitional process, and being ready for a new role when it is your turn to transition. Ecclesiastes 3: 1 says, *"To everything there is a season, and a time to every purpose under the heaven."*

Lois Bradford, a member of Zion Missionary Baptist Church recalls vividly when I announced my retirement. "That season ended in the year 2010. After 45 years of pastoring Zion, our beloved, yet humble Pastor, the Rev. Dr. J.C. Wade, Jr. announced in February that he would be retiring. When Pastor Wade, Jr. said he would be stepping down in October, disbelief and shock were felt throughout the church. From the young to the not so young, and to the seasoned saints, tears flowed and crying was heard throughout the church. We had been blessed by the best for 45 years and it was hard to let go. What flowed through my mind was the question, how could he ever be replaced and by whom? 'You just don't replace a living legend.' The church sighed, moaned, cried and just sat still. We knew that our pastor was hurting telling this to us, but we knew there was a purpose and plan to everything that Pastor Wade did at Zion. There was calmness in his speaking voice as he continued that night. Pastor Wade Jr. went on to say that in addition to him retiring, he was asking the church membership to accept Rev. Charles L. Thompson, Jr. as our new pastor."

Ms. Lois Bradford went on to discuss how the church was being prepared for its new season as she stated, "As difficult as it was to accept Pastor Wade, Jr.'s announcement, some things we didn't know, but what we did know was that under the leadership of Pastor Wade. Jr., we knew he had prayed about it, and God had spoken to him saying it was what Zion needed. Hebrews 11: 1-2 says, *"Now faith is the substance of things hoped for, the evidence of things not seen. For by it the elders obtained a good report."* We knew that God ordained this move and we as members of Zion trusted in God."

In choosing a successor, the retiring pastor has the ability to reassure the congregation that it will not be left leaderless or in the hands of someone who does not understand the church's culture or its needs. By assisting in the selection of a new pastor and embracing that pastor's new role, a church is able to breathe and begin its transition. Ms. Lois Bradford discussed how the church prayed that night to uphold Pastor Wade, Jr. as well as Rev. Thompson, Jr. "We knew it would not be easy, but Proverbs 3: 5-6 says, *"Trust in the Lord with all thine heart; and lean not unto thine own understanding. In all thy ways acknowledge him and he shall direct thy paths,"* This is what Zion did that night. We did not lean unto our own understanding, but we left it to God. It was hard, but we knew it was best to stay focused and keep the love of God and Zion in our hearts. So, the transition was smooth and the church said, 'Amen.' On this historic night we accepted God's plan for our church to continue as one.

SEIZE THE MOMENT

1. When you first retire take two weeks off.
2. Develop a hospital ministry.
3. Development a prison/jail ministry.
4. Be a mentor.
5. Develop a special ministry that allows you to do what you do best.
6. Allow your pastor to help you identify where you can best be used in the ministry.
7. Let your gift make room for you.
8. Develop family time.
9. Develop a hobby.
10. Find something you enjoy doing.
11. Develop a ministry for the nearby seniors citizen complex.
12. Develop some "Me" time.
13. Visit other churches, other than to preach.
14. Get involved in other civic and community affairs.
15. Be an active member of your local ministers alliance, conference, district, state, national, or non-domination work.

The "How" of Transition

"Be careful for nothing; but in every thing by prayer and supplication with thanksgiving let your requests be made known unto God,"
(Philippians 4:6).

We are not defined by a title (Pastor), but by our ministry. The Kingdom of God is our ministry. We must remember that the Kingdom of God is bigger than our title or position as pastor. Being blessed with a title should not give us a "spirit of entitlement." Instead, we must remind ourselves that we are granted the role of pastor because God has chosen to allow us to have it. Pastoring is more than just filling a number of years. It is fulfilling the will of God. It is about your ministry meeting the needs of the church and community. When we have fulfilled God's purpose for us in the role of pastor, we must begin to prepare for transitioning from this role just as we prepared to take it. There are only three acceptable ways to prepare for retirement: The Lord's way, The Lord's way, and The Lord's way!

Appropriate transitioning means that we must have a clear understanding of the role of the pastor, the church and officers from a biblical perspective. In that we are a Bible-believing and Bible-practicing church, we must utilize it in all of our decision-making. The Bible is the Word of God. It is God's written revelation to man. In our "Affirmation of Faith", we announce our belief that the Bible is the absolute authority of the inspired scriptures. "We believe the Holy Bible was written by men divinely inspired, and is a perfect treasure of heavenly instruction; that it has God for its Author, salvation for its end, and truth, without any mixture of error for its matter; that it reveals the principles by which God will judge us; and therefore is, and shall remain to the end of the world, the true basis of all Christian union, and the supreme standard by which all human conduct, creeds, and opinions should be tried." Baptists still believe Paul's writing, that *"every scripture inspired of God is also profitable for teaching, for reproof, for correction, for instruction which is in righteousness: that the man of God may be complete, furnished completely unto every good work,"* (II Timothy 3:16-17, American Standard Version).

We accept the Bible as God's Word. What it teaches is right, what it enjoins we must do, what it prohibits we must not do. By this Bible, all human conducts, creeds, and opinions are to be tried. God's Word, like himself, is eternal and unchangeable. The Bible is a prayer book, and when we let it direct our prayers we actually pray with an inspired vocabulary. When we pray based on the word of God, we communicate with God in His own Words. Only a pastor with virtue and vision can lead a people in transition to higher ground. Such a pastor has something to offer. God has placed us where we are because he wants something magnificent to happen there. God wants us to trust him in our impossible limitations; so, he can bless us with supernatural opportunities. A pastor aiming for a successful transition knows that he must wait on God and then listen when he receives his orders. Even though one might believe that he has "more to give" in his role as pastor, when God makes it clear that the transition period is to begin, we must listen. Remember that our God is never late and never early. He is always right on time and in time. When we listen to God's order for us to move on from pastoring, we can also know that he will assist us in successfully doing so. Isaiah 40:31 reminds us that *"But they that wait upon the Lord shall renew their strength; they shall mount up with wings as eagles; they shall run, and not be weary; and they shall walk, and not faint."* We must keep our connection with the Lord, and sometimes that means He has to re-work us as we wait on Him. The word "wait" in Hebrew is *Homo Phonous* (homo - like; and phono - sound). It means to bind together by twisting; to be gathered together, to be joined, to receive another kind of strength, to merge, and no longer be distinctive.

When we wait on God we are no longer distinctive. We are no longer ourselves. When we wait we merge with God, not by human desperation, but by divine invitation. Waiting is not the last resort, but our first resource. When we merge with God, we are bound together by twisting, we are gathered together to receive another kind of strength. We can now fellowship and communicate with God, not because we desire or deserve it, but because God has declared it. We don't have to produce it because God has already provided it through Jesus Christ. I can now embrace it, express it, and enjoy it.

My nephew Rev. Melvin Wade, Jr., whose father is the pastor of Mt. Moriah Baptist Church in Los Angeles, California, refers to the first chapter of the Book of Joshua when looking at leadership transition. He reminds us that before transition took place, God always spoke to the successor before the predecessor died and went off the scene. For example, according to scripture, God buries his leader Moses. Israel has finished mourning for Moses and now God speaks to Joshua concerning his responsibilities as the new leader of the Nation of Israel. God had chosen Joshua to be Moses' successor as far back as the Battle of Amalek. Exodus

17: 8-16: *(8) "Then came Amalek, and fought with Israel in Rephidim." (9) "And Moses said unto Joshua, Choose us out men, and go out, fight with Amalek: tomorrow I will stand on the top of the hill with the rod of God in mine hand." (10) "So Joshua did as Moses had said to him, and fought with Amalek: and Moses, Aaron, and Hur went up to the top of the hill." (11) "And it came to pass, when Moses held up his hand, that Israel prevailed: and when he let down his hand, Amalek prevailed." (12) "But Moses hands were heavy; and they took a stone, and put it under him, and he sat thereon; and Aaron and Hur stayed up his hands, the one on the one side, and the other on the other side; and his hands were steady until the going down of the sun. "(13) "And Joshua discomfited Amalek and his people with the edge of the sword." (14) "And the* LORD *said unto Moses, Write this for a memorial in a book, and rehearse it in the ears of Joshua: for I will utterly put out the remembrance of Amalek from under heaven." (15) "And Moses built an altar, and called the name of it Jehovah-nissi:" (16) "For he said, Because the* LORD *hath sworn that the* LORD *will have war with Amalek from generation to generation." Even after God had chosen Joshua as the next leader of Israel, He still made it clear that Moses was to lead Joshua's transition.* Moses was given the task to remind Joshua and write it in his book, that Amalek would be exterminated. God then makes it clear that in planning Moses' transition from the leader of Israel, it was imperative that Moses show the people of Israel that he was a part of guiding his successor. In the Book of Numbers, God instructs Moses to ordain Joshua and in Deuteronomy 31:7: *"And Moses called unto Joshua, and said unto him in the sight of all Israel, Be strong and of a good courage: for thou must go with this people unto the land which the* LORD *hath sworn unto their fathers to give them; and thou shalt cause them to inherit it."* Just like Moses, we must not only guide our successors, we must also be there as a support and only want what is best for them. The Bible goes on to show us how Moses gave a final word of blessing and encouragement to his successor Joshua.

Joshua was called of God. Having been called of God, God gives everything including encouragement to Joshua in the following ways:

1. The Promise of the Land (Joshua 1: 2 – 4): *"Moses my servant is dead; now therefore arise, go over this Jordan, thou, and all this people, unto the land which I do give to them, even to the children of Israel. 3) Every place that the sole of your foot shall tread upon, that have I given unto you, as I said unto*

Moses. (4) From the wilderness and this Lebanon even unto the great river, the river Euphrates, all the land of the Hittites, and unto the great sea toward the going down of the sun, shall be your coast."

2. The Promise of His Presence (Joshua 1: 5): *"There shall not any man be able to stand before thee all the days of thy life; as I was with Moses, so I will be with thee: I will not fail thee, nor forsake thee."*

3. The Assurance that God will keep His word, (Joshua 1:6): *"Be strong and of a good courage; for unto this people shalt thou divide for an inheritance the land, which I swear unto their fathers to give them."*

God will give us a promise, but we have to trust Him in the fulfillment. It is by faith. We must stand in faith in spite of the opposition. Problems will come with the promise. God promised to be with Joshua as He was with Moses. The verbatim shows how God was being faithful to His Word. As God was with Moses; so, He would be with Joshua. "I will not leave you nor forsake you." (verse 5).

The promise is repeated in Joshua 1:5 and given to us in Hebrew 13: 5-6, *"Let your conversation be without covetousness; and be content with such things as ye have: for he hath said, I will never leave thee, nor forsake thee."* (6) *"So that we may boldly say, The Lord is my helper, and I will not fear what man shall do unto me."* Although God may choose us to lead His congregation for a short period of time as He did Moses and then Joshua, we must remember that our leadership is not eternal. Even if we do not want to believe it, we must acknowledge it, and accept it.

For those on the other end of the transition process, those taking the helm as the new pastor, you must remember that God spoke to the predecessor before the successor ever knew that a conversation had taken place. When David was king of Israel, he knew the Temple of God was to be built; yet, not by him. However, David provided the resources for his predecessor, his son Solomon to build the temple. Sometimes in the process of transition, the retiring pastor must understand that although God has a plan for His church, it may not be the retiring pastor's job to fulfill it. Instead, God will reiterate His plan so that the retiring pastor can assist the incoming pastor in accomplishing God's vision for the church. In doing so, God will make sure that the successor was always present when God gave the vision to the predecessor. Whatever the predecessor did not finish, the successor finished because he was always present when the vision was given. When discussing vision, Bishop Joseph Walker, Pastor of Mt. Zion Baptist Church in Nashville, Tennessee says, "Vision under supervision always has God's provision. There will never be a need for revision, and never be a day of division."

Leaders change. Time changes, but God never changes. Too many people spend too much time trying to see how it's going to turn out, when God has already given us the promise as he did with Joshua. The Young's Literal Translation in Joshua 1:3 says, *"Every place on which the sole of your foot treadeth, to you I have given it, as I have spoken unto Moses."* What a promise God gave to Joshua! No one will be able to stand up against you all the days of your life. To reinforce those words, God reminded Joshua of everything His heavenly hand had accomplished through Moses. The secret to Moses' success had been God's presence with him. It would be the secret to Joshua's success also, and it continues to be the secret to every pastor and the church.

When looking at the *How* of Transition, pastors transitioning into retirement must be willing to *re-set, re-work, re-evaluate, re-invent, re-start,* and *refocus.*

Re-set: There must be a time table for retirement.

Re-Work: You are not stopping, you are re-working the field. You are entering into a new field of labor.

Re-Evaluate: You are still in God's Ministry.

Re-Invent: Look at where God wants you to minister.

Re-Start: Look at where you are and where you feel God wants you to go. It will be a new beginning and not an ending.

Re-Focus: On the will of God.

By following these steps, we allow God to work. Remember that retirement simply means that you enter into a second phase of pastoral ministry. In this period of Post-Pastoring in which you are no longer leading a specific church, but instead assisting other pastors and congregations by sharing what God has given to you, you continue to be a blessing for pastors and churches based on your years of experience and your continual walk with God, by faith.

Post-Pastoral Ministry

As a retired pastor, you must be sensitive to the voice of God, through the ministry of the Holy Spirit. Retirement does not mean you go home and sit down and do nothing. God has given us ministries beyond the pastoral ministry. Where once our primary field was the church we pastored and the community in which the church was located, in post-pastoral ministry, **"The World is our field."**

In East Chicago, Indiana where I was pastor at Zion Missionary Baptist Church for 45 years, our Twin City Ministerial Alliance had become inactive. Due to its inactivity, our churches were not able to have the kind of impact we should have as a Christian community. Having transitioned from pastor to Pastor-Emeritus, God placed it in my spirit to call the pastors in the community and share with them the need for our ministerial alliance to be reorganized and revitalized. The response was overwhelming and we began to meet at Zion Missionary Baptist Church, where Rev. Dr. Charles L. Thompson, Jr. had succeeded me as pastor. God used us to recommend and initiate a "City-wide revival, which has since blessed our pastors, our churches, and the entire city. Through these revivals we are now revived, motivated, renewed, and united as never before to carry out the mission and the mandate of the Master. In my post-pastoral ministry, I began living and assisting the ministerial alliance in God's directive found in St. Matthew 28: 18-20, *"And Jesus came and spake unto them, saying, All power is given unto me in heaven and in earth. Go ye therefore, and teach all nations, baptizing them in the name of the Father, and of the Son, and of the Holy Ghost: Teaching them to observe all things whatsoever I have commanded you: and, lo, I am with you always, even unto the end of the world."* As retired pastors, we can still use what God has given us to bring about change.

In retirement, we must be convinced that God is not going to waste our time. If we are where God wants us to be in ministry, we must ask him to fulfill his purpose in us while there. God knows who we are and will accomplish His will in our lives, but only when we have been faithful to the one that has been given authority over us. We must remember that God elevates the faithful even in retirement. Even if we do not see ourselves as the leaders of congregations anymore, we are still called to support others in God's work. Even the famed Academy Award's Oscar is awarded to supporting actors. We must concentrate on being faithful and not famous. "Fame is fleeting, but faithful is forever." As pastors in retirement, we are to help people see what faithfulness really means.

In 1972, after attending the National Baptist Congress of Christian Education with my father Rev. Dr. J.C. Wade Sr. and mother Mrs. Mary Frazier Wade, my father took me to the Ministers' Division where Rev. Dr. Reedie Moore was to deliver the Devotional Message. At the time he was to deliver his message, Rev. Dr. Moore became ill. At the recommendation of my father, I was asked to deliver the devotional message, along with a dear friend and colleague, Rev. Dr. Cullen Hill of Greater Concord Missionary Baptist Church in Detroit, Michigan. The following year, we were asked to be on standby in case Rev. Dr. Moore was too ill to travel. The next year, Rev. Dr. Moore was finally able to deliver the devotional message, but because of our spirit of humility and faithfulness, Rev. Dr. Hill and I didn't get upset because we could not preach. Instead, we were grateful for being asked to standby for Dr. Moore. The next year Dr. Moore could not preach and Rev. Dr. Hill and I were once again asked to preach the devotional message at the National Baptist Congress of Christian Education. At that time, the Director said that it was due to our spirit of humility and faithfulness that they wanted us to continue providing the message each year. I am forever grateful for the God-given opportunity to serve in this capacity for 35 years. This is just one of many moments in which I learned that if you are faithful to God, He will be faithful to you. God rewards faithfulness.

The word *Selah* in the Bible means an *interlude*. It is a musical or liturgical sign. It is a pause in the music to make a transition in the theme or composition. It means to pause and think. Before retirement, God gives us a *Selah* moment; a pause to transition. In the midst of our *Selah* moment, God reminds us that he is our provider and our provision.

Thus far, we have focused on the spiritual aspects of the *How* to transition. However, retirement requires preparation not only spiritually, but also physically. It is just as important for retiring pastors to understand the importance of financial planning as it is for anyone else getting ready to make that transition. Rev. Dr. Julius Scruggs, President of the National Baptist Convention USA, Inc. and Senior Pastor of First Missionary Baptist Church in Huntsville, Alabama presents a short video on the National Baptist Convention USA, Inc. website about the importance of pastors and church employees having retirement plans. Rev. Dr. Scruggs speaks as an advocate for the partnership between the National Baptist Convention USA, Incorporated, and the Ministers and Missionaries Benefit Board (MMBB) retirement plan for pastors and church employees. Rev. Dr. Scruggs said that pastors and church employees need financial security just as any other person who works in any industry. His video message on the importance of pastors preparing for retirement can be viewed on the National Baptist Convention USA, Incorporated, website: www.nationalbaptist.com/resources.

At times, we cringe when the church is compared to corporate America. We want to argue that the church is solely to be "The Church" and that we must not treat it as a business. Yet, in the same breath, we talk about "Going about the Lord's work, doing God's business." We also talk about ministry life as a vocation, which is nothing more than

> At times, we cringe when the church is compared to corporate America. We want to argue that the church is solely to be "The Church" and that we must not treat it as a business. Yet, in the same breath, we talk about "Going about the Lord's work, doing God's business."

another word for profession, occupa-tion, or career. Pastors are often expected to devote themselves to the needs of the congregation, often making it their primary work. In the private sector, within the first 90 days of employment, we are called in to complete forms related to retirement planning. We hear terms like 403b, 401k, etc. and are encouraged to think about our last day of employment on what is truly our first day. Like in any other occupation, the pastor and the church must plan for the financial needs of the pastor before he moves towards retirement. Depending on your individual circumstances and that of your church, it is sometimes best to begin with a simple plan that is workable for you and the church. If for some reason the church is not in agreement or equipped to assist you with a financial package for retirement, then you must work on one for yourself. Every church, if possible needs to develop a retirement plan for the pastor, which can be a part of the overall package created for him when he takes on the responsibility as pastor.

As stated previously, if the church is not able to offer you a retirement package, you will need to set a plan in place for yourself as soon as you become pastor. Met-Life indicates the three stages of retirement are: 1) saving for retirement, 2) nearing retirement, and 3) in retirement. The *How* of transition as it relates to financial planning is for you to be prepared for stage three (**In Retirement**). Sit down with a bank financial counselor and/or investment planner who you can work with on a regular basis. Begin with a basic savings account, including possible investments in Certificates of Deposit (CD's) a 401-K, stocks and bonds. There are a plethora of well-known and respected companies that offer retirement and investment packages. A few of those companies are highlighted below. The National Baptist Convention USA, Inc. Retirement Program in partnership with the Ministers and Missionaries Benefit Board (MMBB) is designed specifically for pastors and church employees.

• National Baptist Convention U.S.A., Inc. Retirement Program in partnership with the Ministers and Missionaries Benefit Board (MMBB) offer retirement plans. These plans are all tax-deferred, offer lifetime retirement income and the opportunity to invest in a range of investment options. With a 100-year track record and backed by the expertise of a professional investment committee and fund managers, MMBB has a sound investment strategy. Flexible payment options are available. Medical and dental insurance plans for those in active ministry are available from MMBB. These plans help churches and faith-based institutions attract and keep valued clergy and lay staff members. The retirement, health, death and disability benefits plans protect churches in the event of a catastrophic illness or death to the minister and other staff members.

• New York Life offers several retirement options for planning your future. This message resonates on their website, "The old cliché applies: "people don't plan to fail; they fail to plan." According to New York Life, "planning is not always fun, and in today's world it's often hard to find the time. After more than 168 years, we can say with confidence those who do never regret it. And when it comes to planning your financial future now is always the best time to start." No matter how young of a pastor you are, it is never too early to begin planning for your retirement.

• Waddell & Reed is an asset management and financial planning firm, which provides proven investment and planning services to individuals and institutional investors.

• Metropolitan Life (Met-Life) can help you assess, calculate, and effectively address your retirement future. Their retirement strategy takes you step-by-step through the significant phases of retirement planning, such as envisioning your retirement, determining what retirement will cost, funding your retirement, and protecting your retirement income.

• Nationwide Financial offers financial options such as IRAs (aka Individual Retirement Accounts) as a "popular method of do-it-yourself investing. An IRA is a personal investment plan that is designed to help all kinds of people saves for retirement. According to Nationwide Financial, as long as you earn taxable income such as wages, salaries, fees, tips, bonuses, commissions and taxable alimony, you can contribute.

As President of the National Baptist Convention USA, Inc., Rev. Dr. Scruggs continues to advocate for pastoral retirement planning. As a young man growing up with a father who pastored for over 50 years, Rev. Dr. Scruggs said that he never heard his father talk about a retirement plan. Rev. Dr. Scruggs is quick to point out that when he first went into ministry, retirement was not on his mind. Yet, looking back he wishes it had been because he would have been more prepared at an earlier age.

I believe that pastors need to understand finances by being <u>systematic</u>, <u>consistent</u>, and <u>prompt</u>. Even if they are unable to assist initially and the pastor must start retirement planning on his own, churches should work diligently to ensure the financial stability of the pastor during retirement. We can no longer take planning for retirement lightly, nor can we discount the need for young pastors to start planning the moment they began pastoring. To address this need, our Twin-City Ministerial Alliance in East Chicago, Indiana has developed a retirement savings program through Centier National Bank to assist pastors.

"When the church blesses the man of God, the result is a "blessing fall-out." In other words, when the church assists in planning for the financial stability of its pastor after he finishes serving them, God pours out His blessings on the entire church congregation.

Whether it's spiritual, physical, or financial, when faced with that important question - How does a pastor transition into retirement?" There is actually a very simple answer – the Word of God. Even though this book serves as a supplemental guide to transitioning from pastoring to a post-pastoral ministry, it is solely a supplement. It is not intended to take the place of the will of God. If you really want to know how to make the transition and be in the will of God, you MUST read the Word of God (The Bible) and like Nike says, "Just Do it." If you want to know if God will keep you after your pastoral ministry, read the Bible. When the servant of God obeys and trusts the Word of God, he need not fear failure. Rev. Donaldson Jones, Special Assistant to the President of the National Baptist Convention USA, Inc. in his 2012 message to the Ministry Division said, "The Bible is not a funny book, a fantasy book, a feeble book, a fashionable book, a fatherless book, or a fleshly book, it is God's book."

The retiring and incoming pastor must seek God's will not only for himself, but for the congregation as well. Transitioning from one leader to another can be a season of challenges for the church, but when pastors seek the will of God every step of the process, they can then impart Godly wisdom into the congregation and the result is a smooth transition. Jeremiah 3:15,*"And I will give you pastors according to mine heart, which shall feed you with knowledge and understanding."* Acts 20:28, *"Take heed therefore unto yourselves, and to all the flock, over the which the Holy Ghost hath made you overseers, to feed the church of God, which he hath purchased with his own blood."*

The "Hope" of Transition

"There shall not any man be able to stand before thee all the days of thy life; as I was with Moses, so I will be with thee: I will not fail thee, nor forsake thee,"
(Joshua 1:5).

The *Hope of Transition* for a retiring pastor and congregation is that God provides not only His God-sent successor, but also a smooth transition for the spiritual stability of the church.

When I became pastor of Zion Missionary Baptist Church, I was a young man, but all of my fellowship was with older pastors and ministers who helped mentor me by shaping and molding my pastoral and preaching ministries. As I grew older, I realized that many of the pastors and ministers who had started their pastoral careers at the same time as I had moved away, some passed away, some became incapacitated, and still some were in nursing homes. I discovered that when you are younger, your friends and associates are numerous, but as you get older they diminish. The platform narrows. It narrows when you get older because the number of pastors, ministers and friends you start out with begin to shrink. Whether through sickness, relocation, or death, your circle of friends will decrease. I began to invest in younger pastors and preachers (not getting rid of the old). During revivals and special days, I would ask younger pastors to come and preach. Now, that I am retired the investment has paid off. During the course of the

93

year, I do a lot of preaching and most of it is done for younger preachers/pastors that I have helped and invested in their ministries. By making a connection with younger pastors before, during, and after my transition to retirement, I was able to demonstrate the importance of continuing to utilize the wisdom of elder pastors. It is important that pastors make some investments in young people. When they get older and are out of the pastoral ministry, too many pastors are lonely and alone. When you make no investment in people it translates into little or no investment in the Kingdom of God. Kingdom investment will pay dividends much greater than money. Young people are the face of our future. They have value and importance and the only limits are the ones we place upon them by not offering guidance as they navigate what it means to be a Christian. When you build a ladder with youth, you build a ladder for everyone to climb. It is always my hope and prayer that what I invest in young pastors and preachers is remembered as the wisdom which God allows me to impart into their ministry.

Rev. Chet J. Johnson, Sr., Pastor of the New Tabernacle Missionary Baptist Church in Gary,

Indiana was one who affirms the benefit of having older pastors offer advice and guidance. He recounts his experience growing up at Zion Missionary Baptist Church during the 45-years I pastored there. Pastor Johnson said, "I became a member of the Zion Missionary Baptist Church at the age of 11 in November 1965, which was the same year Pastor Wade came to Zion. As I look back over my ministry life and review all the steps from 11 years old to the present, Pastor J. C. Wade Jr. has always been there. When I say that he has been there I mean that he has been "hands on" there, and I realize with all certainty that this relationship was not only God-designed but also God-assigned."

Pastor Johnson went on to discuss the importance of not only offering guidance, but opportunities within the church. He stated, "Pastor Wade gave me my first assignment to pray in a public forum as a Junior Deacon (when we prayed bowed knee and leaning on a chair). Pastor Wade gave me my first Sunday school teaching assignment in the Youth Department as an assistant to Mrs. Thelma Phillips, and I was no more than 13 years old."

Even as younger ministers leave churches to further their ministry, increase their education, etc., older pastors and specifically those who are moving towards transition, must be steadfast in providing them with new challenges associated with pastoral leadership.   Pastor Johnson discussed how, "throughout my life, Pastor Wade had involved me in ministry in some form or another. When I went off to college there was a break in my church involvement at Zion as well as with Pastor Wade, but after college my involvement continued. I was given more Sunday School assignments, themes to speak on, and even as a layperson, I was given the opportunity to speak on Men's Day from behind the sacred pulpit.   While speaking at Men's Day I accidentally said, 'I want to thank Pastor Wade for allowing me to **preach** on this subject,' although I meant to say **speak.** God does have a sense of humor too."

In offering hope in the transition, pastors must support the gifts of new ministers/pastors. Transitioning pastors must be a guide and role model during this time. Pastor Johnson looked at his own role as successor of New Tabernacle Missionary Baptist Church as a good one, as he noted: "I could go on and on about how much Pastor Wade has meant to me, and continues to in my ministry as well as life in general, but that would be a book by itself. Pastor Wade accepted my calling to the ministry, licensed me in the ministry, ordained me in my ministry, and allowed me to be at his home when I received the call from New Tabernacle Missionary Baptist Church accepting me as their pastor. Pastor Wade was even with me when I made my first hospital visit as a pastor."

In having an active role in the transition process, retiring pastors are able to connect with the new pastor within their church. If done correctly, this connection will transcend the church and the pulpit. Pastor Johnson discussed how such a process unfolded with me. "My grandfather, Rev. Thornton Smith, Sr., who also served as a father-figure to me, was a close friend to Pastor Wade. My grandfather was alive when I received my calling to the ministry under Pastor Wade. I will never forget him instructing me to follow Pastor Wade closely and by doing that, I would be alright. The greatest moment I experienced in my ministry relationship with Pastor Wade Jr. was when he asked me to be his best man as he and Mrs. Wade renewed their marriage vow for their 50th Anniversary Celebration. My immediate thought was that it couldn't get any better than that. As a matter of fact, it is a testament that this relationship is more than ministry, it is personal."

The relationship of Pastor Johnson, his pastoral leadership, as well as I, is an example of how hope and prayers have paid off. It pays to serve Jesus, and it pays to serve him every day. Not only did I invest in young pastors and preachers, but also I became a non-denominational pastor, embracing the relationship of other pastors as long as they preached the Gospel of Jesus Christ. My main concerns for denominations other than Baptist was did they know Jesus as Savior? Were they saved, sanctified, and filled with the Holy Spirit? Were they a Bible-believing and Bible practicing church? If the answers were positive, I was confident the fellowship was real. Now I have opportunities to preach to other denominations other than Baptist. The gospel is for the "whosoever!" John 3:16-17:

"For God so loved the world, that he gave his only begotten Son, that whosoever believeth in him should not perish, but have everlasting life. For God sent not

his Son into the world to condemn the world; but that the world through him might be saved." St. Mark 16: 15-16, *"And he said unto them, Go ye into all the world, and preach the gospel to every creature. He that believeth and is baptized shall be saved; but he that believeth not shall be damned."*

We are right to express hope in the transition process. Rev. Kelly Williams, Pastor of the Greater Destiny Bible Church in East Chicago Indiana states that "an indelible theme that runs through the Bible is God's plan of succession. One of the hidden truths recorded in scripture is that God always has a plan of succession when it pertains to His program. As a pastor having been groomed by the leadership of Pastor Wade, I learned that God never presents what we are not prepared for. The church must be willing to embrace this principle if it is to minister to the next generation of believers. I have experienced personally the pains of pastoring parishioners who were not prepared for succession."

Pastor Kelly states that God's method of succession is displayed throughout the Bible. When Adam sinned God had a plan of succession and covered Adam until the second Adam (Jesus) showed up on the scene. John the Baptist prepared the way for Jesus and while his ministry was growing and thriving, he constantly reminded his followers "there is another who will come after me of whose shoes I am not worthy to fill."

When Moses knew that he had forfeited the privilege of leading his people into Canaan and that he would die before they made their entrance, he asked God to name his successor so that his people would not be as sheep that have no shepherd. Numbers 27: 15-23, *"And Moses spake unto the Lord, 'saying, (16) Let the Lord, the God of the spirits of all flesh, set a man over the congregation, (17) Which may go out before them, and which may go in before them, and which may lead them out, and which may bring them in; that the congregation of the Lord be not as sheep which have no shepherd. (18) and the Lord said unto Moses, Take thee Joshua the son of Nun, a man in whom is the spirit, and lay thine hand upon him; (19) And set him before Eleazar the priest, and before all the congregation; and give him a charge in their sight. (20) And thou shalt put some of thine honour upon him, that all the congregation of the children of Israel may be obedient. (21) And he shall stand before Eleazar the priest, who shall ask counsel for him after the judgment of Urim before the Lord: at his word shall they go out, and at his word they shall come in, both he, and all the children of Israel with him, even all the congregation. (22) And Moses did as the Lord commanded him: and he took Joshua, and set him before Eleazar the priest, and before all the congregation: (23) And he laid his hands upon him, and gave him a charge, as the Lord commanded by the hand of Moses.* God's choice was Joshua whom he described in verse 18 as *a man in whom is the spirit.* Joshua was sovereign-appointed, but he was not to forget the one he succeeded. Moses was moved with gratitude to God to know that his leadership would be perpetuated through Joshua, and when Moses laid his hand upon him the children of Israel harkened unto him. Deuteronomy 34:9, *"And Joshua the son of Nun was full of the spirit of wisdom; for Moses had laid his hands upon him: and the children of Israel hearkened unto him, and did as the Lord commanded Moses."*

If men such as Moses, Elijah, Apostle Paul, and most importantly Jesus Christ had plans for succession and carried them out, who are we to not make plans? We do God's people a disservice when we have no plan of succession. We should do our best to train successors to take over when we move on. In their lesson on Biblical succession, The Reaching through Teaching Ministries emphasizes, "The disciples' success after Jesus departed proves that leadership can be passed on by investing in a plan for succession. Good stewardship includes preparing for the time when a leader will no longer lead."

Two years before my retirement, I prayed and God put in my spirit to ask Rev. Dr. Charles L. Thompson, Jr., who at the time was Pastor of Metropolitan Baptist Church in Gary, Indiana, to join me at Zion Missionary Baptist Church as Executive Assistant to the pastor. As my Executive Assistant, Pastor Thompson Jr. came and presented his vision to us for the church. Our church saw in him the anointing of the Holy Spirit, and we accepted him. Pastor Thompson Jr. worked diligently with us in ministry including preaching, teaching, new membership orientation, outreach, evangelism, and hospital visitation.

Our church leaders were so impressed with Pastor Thompson, Jr.'s leadership and spiritual commitment that they agreed and gave their support in favor of Pastor Thompson, Jr. coming to our church.   It was important for us as a church to dignify Pastor Thompson, Jr.'s position; therefore, he was given an office and stipend to support him and his family.

While serving as Executive Assistant, Pastor Thompson Jr. immersed himself fully by assisting and supporting me. He shared his vision of church growth with the leadership at Zion Missionary Baptist Church.   As part of Pastor Thompson, Jr.'s vision for spiritual growth, he presented his plan for the "Rev. Dr. & Mrs. J.C. Wade, Jr. Spiritual Growth and Church Development Conference," which took place for three nights in February 2009.   The conference focus was faith, family, fellowship, and finances.   Scripture references for the conference were: (Faith: *"Now faith is the substance of things hoped for, the evidence of things not seen,"* (Hebrew 11:1).

- Family: *"And ye shall hallow the fiftieth year, and proclaim liberty throughout all the land unto all the inhabitants thereof: it shall be a jubilee unto you: and ye shall return every man unto his possession, and ye shall return every man unto his family,"* (Leviticus 25:10).

- <u>Fellowship</u>: *"But if we walk in the light, as he is in the light, we have fellowship one with another, and the blood of Jesus Christ his Son cleanseth us from all sin,"* (I John 1:7).

- <u>Finance</u>: *"Bring ye all the tithes into the storehouse, that there may be meat in mine house, and prove me now herewith, said the Lord of hosts, if I will not open you the windows of heaven, and pour you out a blessing, that there shall not be room enough to receive it,"* (Malachi 3:10).

The objective of the conference was to spiritually equip the saints to do ministry in the 21st Century, and help develop the saints to take a more active role in church growth efforts. The four main areas of membership that the conference focused on were children, teens, young adults, and seniors. During the conference achievements were established for each age group as a means to attain adequate spiritual, social, and physical development; thus increasing the spiritual growth and development in the church. For example, in the children's group ages 6 – 9 years old, the achievements needed to increase adequate development for growth included:

- Increase physical skills necessary to successfully complete childhood games.
- Establishment of wholesome attitudes toward self
- Compatibility with peers
- Social adjustments between boys and girls
- Building values in family, faith, and fellowship
- Importance of consistency in giving (tithes and pastoral support)
- For youth ages 14 – 16 years old, achievements established to increase adequate development were:
- Continued awareness and development of strong traits/abilities
- Improving weaknesses
- Development of self-esteem/self-acceptance
- Achieving emotional independence
- Achieving awareness of economic independence
- Increasing church responsibilities
- Continued importance of Godly respect, self-respect, and respect for others
- Setting short-term/long-term goals
- Methods of executing goals
- Importance of consistency in giving (tithes

and Pastor's support)

Achievements to increase the spiritual, social, and physical development for growth were established for every age group, ranging from children as young as three to seniors 62 years and older.

The conference sought to gain new membership into the church fellowship, and accomplish it by winning souls to Christ, understanding financially how to support the pastor and the church through giving, addressing the need for family worship, teaching the value of faith in our lives, and learning Christian fellowship with one another.

The conference included sessions for young adults led by Pastor Kelly B. Williams of Greater Destiny Baptist Church, East Chicago. Pastor Allen Robinson of New Sardis Missionary Baptist Church, Gary Indiana, led the adult sessions. Pastor Thompson Jr. led the deacons and men of the church session; while Rev. Wade Jr., took the lead on the session for pastors and ministers. Ms. Pearlie Eatman and Ms. Dawn Dawkins, members of Zion, led the intercessors group. The general assembly lecturer for each day was Pastor Chet Johnson, Sr.

from New Tabernacle Missionary Baptist Church, Gary, Indiana.

As the Executive Assistant for the two years preceding my retirement, Pastor Thompson, Jr. had worked side-by-side with me and it was evident to the entire congregation that Pastor Thompson, Jr. was God-sent. With blessings from both the Zion Missionary Baptist Church family, and myself, Rev. Dr. Charles Lee Thompson, Jr. became the pastor after my retirement in October 2010. Just as I had diligently prayed for, God blessed Zion Missionary Baptist Church with a smooth transition; having not gone one day without a leader.

Hope in transition involves not only the recognition that God will help in the identification of a successor and that transitioning pastors must offer guidance to the incoming pastor, but that one must make sure that such things occur in a timely manner and in order. Rev. Melvin Wade, Sr. says that "by my brother stepping aside before it was too late; by preparing himself to step aside; and by putting in place God's choice for his successor, there was no gap in the transition and the mantle being passed. What that did was safeguard the Zion Missionary

Baptist Church from having to deal with satanic and demonic confusion, which result in church division and laity takeover."

As the newly appointed and anointed pastor of Zion Missionary Baptist Church, Pastor Thompson, Jr. continued to immerse himself in the duties and responsibilities that he had been practicing during the transition period. His energy and enthusiasm for taking the church in to its next phase was evident when in the summer of 2011, Pastor Thompson, Jr. created and led the Strategic Teaching & Enrichment Planning (STEP), which was entitled, *Sizzling Summer 2011*. It was a time to *"Tune in June, Praise Him Highly in July, and Soul-Winning: A must in August."* The focus in June was for the congregation to double their efforts in bringing others to church and financial giving. The entire month of July centered on praising God, and in August the entire church concentrated their efforts on winning souls to Christ. Pastor Thompson, Jr. utilized Numbers 13:30, *"And Caleb stilled the people before Moses, and said, Let us go up at once, and possess it; for we are well able to overcome it,"* as the scripture reference for the conference. Pastor Thompson, Jr.'s work is a testament to what happens when new pastors are allowed to learn from their predecessors, while still being encouraged to bring their own vision to the church. The hope in transition is that God will continue taking care of His people when they follow the Biblical examples He set for succession. Zion Missionary Baptist Church continues to grow under Pastor Thompson, Jr. because God answers prayer. James 5:16: *"Confess your faults one to another, and pray one for another that ye may be healed. The effectual fervent prayer of a righteous man availeth much."*

In the meantime, his wife (our daughter) Mrs. LaShonta Thompson who had completed a music degree at Indiana University joined our music ministry and began working alongside Mrs. Ella Wade with the 100-Plus Voice Children's Choir.

As a part of the transition process, part of the hope in transition lies in not only preparing the pastor, but his wife to serve in the role of First Lady of the church. First-lady Mrs. Thompson said, "One key element to be learned in this position is that the role of the pastor's wife is not to sit on display, but to be willing to serve." Mrs. Thompson learned this as the result of watching her mother Mrs. Ella Wade who served in that capacity for over 50 years. "From birth I have always been able to observe Mrs. Wade as an excellent role-model, wife, mother, friend, daughter, sister, and Christian. She portrayed a woman of wisdom and discernment, learning when to speak and when to be silent. She has been able to demonstrate many characteristics that helped to aid me as first lady. I both welcome and seek counsel from Mrs. Wade on a daily basis realizing the essentiality of not trying to wipe out the foundation, but the need to build on the solid foundation which had already been laid."

A CONGREGATION'S HOPE FOR TRANSITION

In his movie, *Act like a Lady, Think like a* Man, Steve Harvey said a woman needs to know if a man has a plan for her or is he just coming to play. This same mindset is that when a church gets ready for transition, the church needs to know from the incoming pastor if he has a plan and vision, and he is not just coming to play (coming for show and fashion, but not for ministry).

Pastoral change can be very difficult for the membership, especially when the retiring pastor has served in that capacity for so many years. A change in leadership can potentially be one of the most devastating events that can happen, especially in the church; therefore, Godly preparation is crucial. Deacon Larry and Sister Yvette Chafen from Zion Missionary Baptist Church said, "This (Zion) is a full gospel church, where the Bible has been taught. We have been taught that it's all about God. We are a Bible-based church where we believe in the power of prayer. It is the truth. This is the reason why we did not have problems and division when Pastor Wade, Jr. gave us what God had given him."

George Gaddie, a Deacon at Zion Missionary Baptist Church remembers when I began talking about retirement in 2008. He knew it was a serious time in the life of the church. He and the other deacons were called on to pray. They were also called to read and study the Word of God. Deacon Gaddie said, "The question we needed to answer was what would God have us, the pastor and people to do? We did not trust ourselves to make the decision, but we trusted God based on His Word in Proverbs 3: 5-6,' *Trust in the LORD with all thine heart; and lean not unto thine own understanding." (6) 'In all thy ways acknowledge him, and he shall direct thy paths'* Pastor Wade, Jr. made it crystal clear and he shared the question he had to ask himself, 'Do I want to hold on to the church and let it fall, or let go for its future?' As a deacon for the past 18 years, I believe through prayer, that Pastor Wade, Jr. made the right decision to let go. And now that we have our new pastor, Rev. Charles L. Thompson, Jr. we are moving on. I had a personal relationship with Pastor and Sister Wade, which allowed me to know them from a personal stand point, through sharing with them in their home as well as the church. When I came to Zion Missionary Baptist Church as a 17-year-old, I was unable to read, but through 30 years of teaching by Pastor Wade, Jr., God allowed me to read and study His Word, and now I understand the Word of God for myself. Now, I read the Bible in Bible Class, Sunday School, and Baptist Training Union (B.T.U.). This understanding of the Bible gives me a reason to say what I have said. I am at the church daily as one of the custodians, and because of my daily activities and my responsibility, I am able to see first-hand that our church is moving on."

I understood the spiritual necessity to seek counsel from God through prayer for his successor. Churches without a leader for any length of time are vulnerable to Satan's attack on the entire congregation, but the *Hope of Transition* is that God cares and provides for His people, and He knows exactly what we need. Zion Missionary Baptist Church has not missed a beat since Pastor Thompson, Jr. became the under-shepherd, and that occurred only because of the power of God through prayer.

The "Health" of Transition

"Now also when I am old and greyheaded,
O God, forsake me not; until I have shewed
thy strength unto this generation, and thy
power to every one that is to come,"
(Psalms 71:18).

W hen you sense that the Church's progression is becoming stagnant under your leadership, you realize that your pastoral energy is not at the level it needs to be. . The execution of God's vision cannot be accomplished when your enthusiasm has waned and those within church leadership only support out of respect or obligation. When one or both of these factors occurs, it is important to seek sound counseling from the wisdom of retired pastors to help you ensure that your own retirement happens "with dignity" and "with respect" for the Church and for yourself.

When it came time to begin to plan for my own retirement, I consulted with two pastors my father, Rev. Dr. J.C. Wade, Sr., and my best friend, Pastor Emeritus Rev. Dr. Samuel J. Gilbert Sr. of Houston, Texas. It was my hope that learning from the retirement experiences of others, I could navigate my own in a way that was healthy for the church and myself. At the time of our discussions, Rev. Dr. Gilbert, Sr. served as Pastor Emeritus of Mt. Sinai Baptist Church in Houston where he had been pastor for 36 years (1964 – 2000), and led the church to remarkable growth and Christian influence. Rev.

Dr. Gilbert, Sr. had been dynamic in pastoring Mt. Sinai, but also as a leader within the community during and after that time. Rev. Dr. Gregory Ballard shared sentiments about Rev. Dr. Gilbert, Sr. from pastors across Houston and the nation. "Rev. Dr. Gilbert, Sr. gives leadership to the Houston Metropolitan Ministers Conference. Under his visionary leadership as founder and president, this ministry conference attracts several hundred ministers and pastors for the precise purpose of honing and sharpening ministers and ministries in the Greater Houston, Texas area. From preachers with thousands of members to preachers with only a handful, and those without congregations, it is amazing to see preachers and pastors come together and work collaboratively for the good of the Kingdom and community. Although this Baptist Ministers Conference is located in Houston, the influence of these ministers and ministries transcend Houston's boundaries having international and global impact."

When a pastor retires, it not only has significance for him and the congregation he serves, but also for his wife. I cannot emphasize enough the importance of your spouse in the health of your transition into retirement. Proverbs 18:22 says, *"When a man finds a wife, he finds a good thing and obtains favor from the Lord."* My wife, Mrs. Ella "Mama" Wade has shared in my ministry for 51 years. While preparing to write this book, I thought it imperative that I talk with her about her views regarding my pastoral transition. In her words, I was reminded of the importance of having a First Lady who understood not only the work of a pastor, but had faith in God's plan as it relates to transitioning from that position. My wife said it best when she noted, "Our God is an awesome God is the words I speak over and over again, but I wonder sometimes if we really understand the significance and meaning of these words. He is just what it says, *an awesome God, who does the impossible.* I have learned over the years from experience to recognize when the Lord speaks." She went on to further emphasize the importance of having a supportive spouse when moving towards retirement when she asserted, "When Rev. J.C. Wade, Jr. told me that the Lord spoke to him and he shared it with me, my only response was if that is what the Lord has put on your heart, then I will pray with you and for you, and I will never interfere with what the Lord has given to you. I will give you all of my support and prayers. I know that God does not make mistakes. He never errors, and when you are a child of God, he will speak to you. Rev. Dr. Wade, Jr. is a child of the King, and he is an anointed, powerful, praying and Bible-believing pastor and man of God. I know he would not have said it if the Lord had not spoken it. As his wife, I had no doubt in my mind that God was preparing him to make this transition. I prayed, *'Thy way O Lord not mine, Thy will be done O Lord, not mine.'* I thank God that Pastor Wade was led by the Holy Spirit, and followed what the Lord said and not man."

As most retiring pastors have spouses, the role that the spouse has played in the ministry cannot be discounted. The spouse of a pastor has an important role as the helpmate for her husband. Just as God equips the pastor for his role, he also equips his spouse. My mother, Mrs. Mary Wade was married to my father Rev. Dr. J.C. Wade, Sr. for 63 years. My mother speaks very seriously when she says God gives us a pastor, and our job is to follow him. "I was blessed to sleep with a pastor for 63 years, and when God spoke to my husband, he was not talking to me and my job was to follow what my husband said God told him to do. Our responsibility is to follow the pastor as he follows Christ and pray for the pastor," said Mrs. Mary Wade. The Bible says, pray for us.

Mrs. Mary Wade, affectionately referred to as ""Mama" Wade" remembers her husband's decision to retire. "After his health began to fail and he could not function the way he used to, my husband made the decision to retire as the Pastor of Salem Baptist Church instead of waiting to be put out," said Mrs. Mary Wade. Before Rev. Dr. Wade Sr. retired, God used him through the power of the Holy Spirit to guide the church in their choice of his successor Pastor Maurice Watson. In my role as his wife, I supported his retirement and his decision to not go back into the pastoral study or sit in the pulpit unless he was asked to preach. I chose to be his champion and support him when he encouraged the congregation to accept and praise the work his successor was doing within the church."

The Church must also respect and understand that not only is the pastor transitioning to retirement, but his spouse is as well and make provisions for her sacrifice and commitment to the pastoral ministry. At my father's home-going celebration, Pastor

Watson announced in his presentation that although the church had an agreement that ""Mama" Wade" would receive half of Rev. Dr. Wade Sr.'s retirement at his death, he was taking a pastoral privilege and instead giving "Mama" Wade 100 percent of Rev. Dr. Wade Sr.'s retirement. After Pastor Watson made that announcement, the entire congregation stood at length, applauding and shouting "Amen." Pastor Watson had not even consulted with the trustees, deacons, or congregation in advance before making his decision. The following Sunday, Pastor Watson exercised another pastoral privilege announcing that every time the grass had to be cut or the snow plowed at the church, that it was to be carried out at "Mama" Wade's house too. "Mama" Wade was given a special parking place and seating at the church. Pastor Watson said that it was in appreciation for the service that Rev. Dr. Wade Sr. and "Mama" Wade had given to the church, and that it does not end simply because the pastor is no longer pastoring. Mrs. Mary Wade continues to talk about how good Salem is to her even today. The Salem Baptist Church, under the able and capable hands of the present and anointed pastor Rev. Dr. Selwyn Q. Bachus, has continued to carry out what started under Pastor Watson. "Mama" Wade loves to talk about how well Rev. Dr. Bachus can preach and how much she thanks him and the Salem Baptist Church for their love and continued support. She never speaks of Rev. Dr. Bachus without saying how much she loves his "sweet" wife. In 2010, after serving as a member since 1944, my mother moved her membership to my brother, Rev. Dr. Melvin Wade, Sr.'s church in Los Angeles, California.

My wife also understood the importance of supporting me during my pastoral ministry. Yet, she also embodies the need for pastor's spouses to be supportive during post-pastoral ministry.

Since my retirement, my wife has informed me that the most frequent questions people ask is how she feels since my retirement, and how she accepts no longer being First Lady. She so eloquently responds, "I feel just like I felt when Rev. J.C. Wade, Jr. was pastor. I am thankful to God for the opportunity to have been the first lady of Zion Missionary Baptist Church. I had my day and it blessed me in many ways. I am as happy as I can be."

Although I clearly can speak on the issues faced by pastors in transition, my wife cautions retired and deceased pastors' wives to not allow Satan to fill them with jealousy, envy, malice, hatred. She further encourages First Ladies in Transition against feelings of being left out and forgotten, becoming mean-spirited and non-supportive of the church and their husband's transition. Failure to be mindful of the traps associated with this transition can result in the First Lady in Transition lacking in fellowship, having a dislike for the new pastor and first lady, speaking evil, and joining with others to gossip about the pastor and family. She warns, "This is the work of the devil, and you are only hurting yourself. Don't create problems for the next pastor and wife; instead continue being productive and supportive of the pastor and first-lady."

As she concludes, my wife states that every pastor should plan for the day he will retire and that the First Lady must assist him in understanding the importance of doing so. "When you have given your best, that's all you can do. Transitioning to retirement is wonderful when you have been a faithful steward of God's Word. I Corinthians 4: 1-2: *"Let a man so account of us, as of the ministers of Christ, and stewards of the mysteries of God."* Moreover it is required of stewards, that a man (and woman) be found faithful.

In this transition period, a first lady must remind her husband of the positive contributions he has made to the church and that his work for God is not done, but simply changing as "When you have given your best and God has sealed and stamped his approval, 'well done,' then you can have assurance knowing that God is pleased. I can hear the songwriter say:

> If when you give the best of your service,
> Telling the world that the Savior has come.
> Be not dismayed when men don't believe you,
> He'll understand and say well done."

Recognition of being fortunate to have served for as long as God deemed necessary must be a part of the reflection that occurs in transition. My wife went on to acknowledge, "It is a blessing how God used Rev Wade, Jr. in this transition, and I thank my husband for following the Holy Spirit. We are truly blessed at Zion Missionary Baptist Church, as we continue to partner in marriage and ministry. We thank God for these 45 years as pastor and First Lady of Zion and now three years as Pastor Emeritus and former First

Lady, but our work is not finished. The mantle has been passed and we also thank God for our new pastor and First Lady, Rev. Dr. & Mrs., Charles L. & LaShonta Thompson, Jr. God did it, and He is an awesome God." Matthew 6:33: *"But seek ye first the kingdom of God and his righteousness; and all these things shall be added unto you."*

For the First Lady assuming the position during transition, trusting in God and supporting her husband is also crucial. First Lady LaShonta Thompson speaks about the importance of trusting God before, during, and after transitioning. "The transitional period was totally led by God. I was born and raised in this church (Zion Missionary Baptist), with close ties to the membership; therefore, during the period in which my husband was seeking God's voice, I was careful not to give my opinion. When asked, I would respond by saying, 'I have no opinion. I think that whatever God said to do is the right decision.' When God called my husband as Pastor, I immediately became submissive to God's will and the leadership of my husband. The key to sharing in ministry is to pray together, work together, make time for each other, and love the membership." Ephesians 3:20, *"Now unto him that is able to do exceeding abundantly above all that we ask or think, according to the power that worketh in us."*

As First Lady Thompson experienced, her husband was permitted to become pastor without being hindered by the Pastor in Transition. Retiring pastors should not try to impose their will and way on the incoming pastor. You cannot try to pastor through the pastor, even though there are times when you feel there are mistakes being made. Your position should be to pray for the pastor.

If you feel there are some things that you need to share with the pastor, do it in such a way that he feels you are not trying to take away what is now his role. . It is easy for a church and the retiring pastor to want to retreat to what is comfortable and known, even if it is not benefitting the church. Yet, it is up to the retiring pastor to remember why he retired and not allow members to bring information that will entice you to come out of retirement. A true transition for the retiring pastor does not involve permitting the congregation to make you pastor *through* the new pastor, or *around* the new pastor. If you feel the Lord has moved you to retire, "then stay retired and like it!" Watch how you receive information and watch how you share information. All of us have influence with members, but use your influence to promote the Kingdom of God through the pastor. The church will only have one pastor at a time, and when you retire you are not it any longer. Think about the following:

1. I have watched people ride horses, one must be in front and one must be behind.
2. When you drive a car there is only one person under the steering wheel; everybody else is either to the side or in the back.
3. On an airplane, there is only one Captain who is the pilot; anybody else is a co-pilot.
4. In the United States, you have only one President; who is the Commander-in-Chief.
5. In states you have only one Governor.
6. In cities, you have only one Mayor.
7. On the ship you have only one Captain.
8. In sports you have only one Head Coach.
9. In a family, you have only one Head.
10. In schools, you have only one Principal.
11. On the job you have only one Boss.
12. In the church there is only one Head.

13. In the military there is only one General.
14. In the courtroom there is only one Judge.
15. In the Police Department there is only one Chief.
16. In the God-head you have only one Head.

No one is saying that your experience and knowledge are not valuable or should not be shared with the new pastor. However, there are ways to share your concerns with the pastor. First, pray for him before you meet with him and then pray with him when you meet with him. Second, share your concerns and give him the privilege to accept or reject them outright. Third, allow him the opportunity to pray about it before making a decision. Remember, he is the new pastor; so, if he does not want to consider your recommendations or take your advice, then respectfully leave it alone. However, your work is not done. Instead, praise God for at least having the new pastor listen to your thoughts. If he chooses to adhere to your advice/recommendations, also have your own private praise session. . "Don't get mad, get glad." Remember to put your ego aside because in reality it is really not about you, but about the Lord using you

For new pastors and those in transition, can I be candid with you? Can I be for real? Can I really tell you the truth? None of us possesses all of the knowledge and skill needed to effectively pastor a church. It is all about God's grace and God's wisdom. James 1:5: *"If any of you lack wisdom, let him ask of God, that giveth to all men liberally, and unbraideth not; and it shall be given him."*

Offering support and advice to a new pastor is a part of mentoring and making a healthy transition for the new pastor, the church, and yourself. Yet, it is important that we allow the new pastor to integrate his vision into the church. Proverbs 29:18 warns us: *"Where there is no vision, the people perish: but he that keepeth the law, happy is he."* As a matter of fact, we as retiring pastors ought to be the number one supporter of the new vision. In our role as champions and mentors for the new pastor, we still have a needed role. Thank God that we are still needed and can be used. God has gifted all of us. We must use our gift to be a blessing and not a burden. I Corinthians 12: 4-7 says *"Now there are diversities of gifts, but the same Spirit."* (5) *"And there are differences of administrations, but the same Lord."*(6) *And there are diversities of operations, but it is the same*

God, which worketh all in all. (7) "But the manifestation of the Spirit is given to every man to profit withal."

One of the tragedies of retirement is to get caught up in the middle of fighting old and new battles between the pastor and people within the congregation. The Lord has promised if we stand still, He will fight our battles. He is our Jehovah-Nissi. The hymnologist writes:

> *"Be not dismayed what-e'er betide, God will take care of you;*
> *Beneath his wings of love abide, God will take care of you.*
> *No matter what may be the test, God will take care of you;*
> *Lean weary one upon His breast, God will take care of you.*
> *God will take care of you, through every day, o'er all the way,*
> *He will take care of you; God will take care of you."*

Just as retiring pastors play a vital role in making transition a healthy process for the new pastor, young pastors are also an integral part of the *health* of a retired pastor's transition. It is unfortunate that so many new pastors do not know how to treat the retired pastor when they assume the pastoral position. Oftentimes, in the eagerness to realize the dream of being appointed pastor, young pastors want to "erase" all reminders that someone was there before them. The first thing they want to do is take the retiring pastor's picture off the wall. They want to (by design) remove all the memories of the previous pastor. They want to act like he has not done anything and that the church began its existence only when the new pastor came. Let me tell you young pastors, there was a pastor there before you got there. You are standing on somebody else's shoulder.

Rev. Maurice Watson, Pastor of Beulahland Bible Church, Macon. Georgia said in an interview given by Rev. H.B. Charles of Shiloh Metropolitan Baptist Church in Jacksonville, Florida that "when you arrive at a new ministry, try not to tear down the previous pastor's legacy; instead embrace the legacy of the former pastor. Be the chief historian of the church and its culture. Take your time before you make changes in the church." He went on to say that new pastors should concentrate on preaching and teaching, which are the ingredients for developing a healthy and balanced church.

The Bible is right when it says in Galatians 6:7: *"Be not deceived; God is not mocked: for whatsoever a man soweth, that shall he also reap."* Be careful how you treat the previous pastor and his wife. He should be held in the highest esteem—respect and love him. Develop a plan for how the church cares for him and his wife. Many young pastors have come into mega-ministries and act as if they are God's gift to the church, instead of the church being gifts to them. They inherit great ministries. They reap what they have not sown. My father once said to me, "Son, there is an old man and old woman on their way to your house. The only way they do not arrive is they die young." My fellow pastors, don't let people in church make you mistreat a previous pastor. Remember that the previous pastor has people who still love him. It has been my experience that the way you treat the previous pastor is the way people will treat you. My father also advised me that, "You get more flies with honey than you do with salt." We have to be careful that, when a pastor becomes older, and is not as productive as he used to be that we don't just tolerate him. Instead, we should *appreciate* and *celebrate* him for being a servant to God and His people.

I don't care how long you pastor a congregation; there are some people in the church that you will never pastor. To be honest, they don't even allow the Lord to lead them. Then there are times when new pastors encounter great difficulties in the church. Perhaps it is because he did some things that were disrespectful and not Christian-like to the outgoing pastor. There is great value and blessings in recognizing the footprints laid by the previous pastor. Don't get so caught up in changing everything of the retired pastor that you begin seeing your pastoral ministry as an opportunity to *be and do better* than the previous pastor. Pastoring is not a competition, but it is instead an opportunity to appreciate and value the wisdom of the retiring pastor, and thank God for it. I don't care how together you may think you are, you don't want to pass up what has been your inspiration. Pastor Johnson, Sr. of New Tabernacle discusses this as he shares his experience with a former elderly member of his church.

"It was during Pastor Wade's appreciation service on May 19, where I was privileged to bring the message, and while making my introduction, the Holy Spirit reminded me of an earlier experience. It was during our Singles Ministry "Walk-a-Thon" which is held every year in September. The event involves walking or running from the church to Gleason Park and back, which is equivalent to about three miles. I decided I would challenge myself and run my two laps alongside Deacon Walter Moore who was at that time about 75 years old, and who ran in the walk-a-thon every year. Deacon Moore was always an inspiration during the race, and I was in awe of his ability to run like that at 75 years old."

Pastor Johnson, Sr. went on to state, "It had been years since I ran such a distance, but I decided to try anyway. As we made it to the park I followed Deacon Moore, running right behind him. We made our first lap and were about one- third of the way into our second one when all of a sudden Deacon Moore stumbled and fell. My mind immediately went into a competitive-mode and I saw it as an opportunity for me to take the lead. I was younger, faster, and besides, I was still on my feet. Everyone at the church who knew Deacon Moore as a runner spoke highly of him and expected him to come in first, but circumstances seemed to play in my favor and it was my time to take full advantage of Deacon Moore's stumbling. Well, I am so glad today that it was not my mind that I listened to but my heart. Whereas, my mind went into a competitive mode, my heart went into a mode of compassion and I remember saying to myself, the reason I decided to run was because of Deacon Moore, and the reason I had even made it this far was because of him. The real value gained from that whole experience was to do what I had been doing at the beginning of the race – following Deacon Moore. So, I needed to finish the race just as I had started it, and I remember thinking that we should *never pass up our inspiration."*

Pastor Thompson, Jr. is the example of how a new pastor should take his position as the new leader. Pastor Thompson, Jr. has always treated Mrs. Wade and me with love and respect. I thank God for Pastor Thompson, Jr. and Zion M. B, Church for always showing their continual love and appreciation to Mrs. Wade and myself.

In one of his writings titled, "The Incoming Pastor to the Outgoing Pastor," Pastor Thompson, Jr., states that the incoming pastor needs to approach the situation through four areas: **prayer, preaching, paying attention to church flow**, and **providing**.

Pray for the blessing of the outgoing pastor. It is not an easy task for an outgoing pastor who has served decades in a church to walk away from the ministry of that congregation. During his tenure, he has established relationships and been an integral part of many of the church experience including conducting baptisms, weddings, and even funerals. Embracing the retiring pastor and continuing to provide spiritual support for him is another required activity of the new pastor seeking a healthy transition. Pastor Thompson discussed how he accomplishes this: "As the incoming pastor of the Zion Missionary Baptist Church, I try to encourage the congregation to set aside weekly prayer for Rev. Dr. Wade, Jr. and his wife; and pray that Rev. Dr. Wade, Jr. and Sister Wade's life is still utilized in the church to take the ministry to a higher level."

Change comes with evolution not revolution. Many times incoming pastors look for things that they can change, or how they can prove their ministry will be better than the outgoing pastor. The incoming pastor needs to embrace what the outgoing pastor has already done. For a healthy transition, new pastors must first focus on the P's of Healthy Transition:

1. Preach
2. Pay Attention
3. Provide for the outgoing pastor

When called to the preaching ministry, the key word is Preach. We must preach the gospel like Paul said in Romans 1: 15-16, *"So, as much as in me is, I am ready to preach the gospel to you that are at Rome also. (16), For I am not ashamed of the gospel of Christ: for it is the power of God unto salvation to everyone that believeth; to the Jew first, and also to the Greek."* Just as it was charged to me that I preach the unadulterated Word of God to the church, it was just as important that the incoming pastor also understood the charge to preach the Word of God.

After continuing to offer spiritual support and love to the outgoing pastor and making sure to remember that the primary responsibility is to continue to preach the gospel, the new pastor must take additional steps to make sure a healthy transition occurs.

Meditate on how you can enhance the ministry with creative ideas that will fit in the flow of the ministry of the church without causing a split or division.

Pay attention to the flow of the church. Learn what direction the church was going under the leadership of the outgoing pastor. Meditate on how you can enhance the ministry with creative ideas that will fit in the flow of the ministry of the church without causing a split or division.

Provide for the outgoing pastor. Remember he has earned it. The outgoing pastor in insuring a healthy transition has demonstrated his unconditional love for the church. In addition, in his role as pastor, he and his family have made sacrifices in order to fully serve the church. At Zion Missionary Baptist Church from which I transitioned, there are things that are in place to provide an ongoing sense of home and hospitality for my wife and I. We still have our reserved parking space, the same office, reserved seating in church. Also, the church established The Rev. Dr. J.C. and Mrs. Wade Jr. Spiritual Growth and Development Conference in our honor. Every year on the third Sunday in May, Pastor Thompson leads the church in an appreciation service honoring the both of us.

My wife and I are so appreciative of the continued spiritual, physical, and financial support shown by Pastor Thompson and the Zion Missionary Baptist Church. Pastor Thompson, Jr. always reminds the church of the investments made through my preaching and teaching ministry. During the year he allows me time to preach, and Mrs. Wade was appointed Executive Consultant of the Music Ministry. Pastor Thompson, Jr. not only supports my retirement in the things he says, but most importantly in the things he does. I am always reminded of the words spoken by Pastor Thompson, Jr. when he said, "Zion's future destiny is determined by how we treat Pastor Wade and Sister Wade." My wife is always saying, "We have a good pastor, and he and the Zion Missionary Baptist Church have been and continue to be good to us."

When churches and leaders fail to trust the pastor for leadership, then their actions and words are nothing more than unloving linguistics prodigy, and loud pompous discordant, ostentatious rhetoric, with lack of purity in thought. However, when leaders and the congregation trust pastoral leadership, as spelled out in the Bible, it will transcend doubt. You are not suspicious or gullible, but you move with honorable intentions to progressive fulfillment in God-given leadership. President Abraham Lincoln once said, "I have been driven to my knees because I had nowhere else to go." Too many pastors and churches have been blustering and blundering in transition; locked in membership and not stewardship trying to do God's will.

When we as pastors realize that the ministry is not about us, but all about God, then it will change our attitude about retirement. We will understand that it is not about what I can get, but what I can give. What is important in the life of every pastor is that **God is pleased.**

Retirement is about trusting God by faith. Many times we hear about "blind faith," but faith is not blind. The Bible is clear in defining faith as shown in several translated versions of Hebrews 11: 1-2:

King James Version:
"Now faith is the substance of things hoped for the evidence of things not seen. For by it the elders obtained a good report."

Common English Bible:
"Faith is the reality of what we hope for, the proof of what we don't see. The elders in the past were approved because they showed faith."

The Message (MSG):
"The fundamental fact of existence is that this trust in God, this faith, is the firm foundation under everything that makes life worth living. It's our handle on what we can't see. The act of faith is what distinguished our ancestors; set them about the crowd."

American Standard Version:

"Now faith is the assurance of things hoped for, a conviction of things not seen. For therein the elders had witness borne to them."

Contemporary English Version (CEV):

"Faith makes us sure of what we hope for and gives us proof of what we cannot see. It was their faith that made our ancestors pleasing to God."

Darby Translation (DARBY):

"Now faith is the substantiating of things hoped for, the conviction of things not seen. For in the power of this the elders have obtained testimony."

Douay-Rheims 1899 American Edition (DRA):

"Now faith is the substance of things to be hoped for, the evidence of things that appear not. For by this the ancients obtained a testimony."

Expanded Bible EXB):

"Faith means being sure (the assurance; or the tangible reality, or the sure foundation) of the things we hope for and knowing that something is real even if we do not see it (the conviction/assurance/evidence about things not seen). Faith is the reason we remember (or God

commended/approved) great people who lived in the past (the people of old; the ancients; our spiritual ancestors)."

Amplified Bible (AMP):

"Now faith is the assurance (the confirmation, the title deed) of the things we hope for, being the proof of things we do not see and the conviction of their reality (faith perceiving as real fact what is not revealed to the senses). For by faith – trust and holy fervor born of) the men of old had divine testimony borne to them and obtained a good report.

Wycliffe Bible (WYC):

"But faith is the substance of things that be to be hoped, and an argument of things not appearing. Forsooth faith is the substance of things to be hoped, an argument, or certainty, of things not appearing. And in this faith old men have gotten witnessing."

Retirement is not about blind faith, but it is based upon faith in God; and faith in God is based upon the Word of God. Isaiah 40: 8 assures us, *"The grass withereth, the flower fadeth: but the word of God shall stand forever."*

When a new pastor and the retiring pastor work to insure a healthy transition, the congregation not only witnesses it, but also feels blessed by the process. Evelyn Forte, a member of Zion Missionary Baptist Church has been in a close relationship with both my wife and I since she became a member in 1966. Our relationship grew even closer as Evelyn became the godmother of our children, Camellia, James, and LaShanta. Evelyn reflects on my retirement with vivid memories. "I was filled with many emotions - sadness, anger, perplexity, and disappointment. I didn't understand why he would retire and leave us. So, in my fleshly thoughts, I decided to withdraw from Pastor and Mrs. Wade. I wanted to wean myself away, but the harder I tried to step away, the more difficult it became. Then, I remember getting quiet and asking God to help me understand retirement. I researched the word and its definition was clear. To retire means to honorably remove oneself from an assigned duty, but retain the title using Emeritus. Retire, much to my disbelief does not mean to become inactive. I learned that Pastor Wade's retiring did not mean to *stop*, but it simply meant to *move forward* with a different objective and mission. Truly, Pastor Wade has proven himself to remain faithful to the finish.

He continues to preach, minister, and aid the body of Christ. I am so grateful to have had such a dedicated man of God lead me on this spiritual walk. May God's continued blessings keep him for years to come."

Deana Johnson, who served as the church administrator for Rev. Wade, Jr. and now Pastor Thompson, Jr. speaks fondly of the five generations of family members, which Rev. Dr. Wade, Jr. served. Ms. Johnson's daughter participated in the youth ministries of the church, particularly the 100-Plus Voice Children's Choir under the direction of former First Lady Mrs. Wade. Ms. Johnson remembers vividly when her daughter Chareice was attending Franklin Elementary School in East Chicago. Chareice's fourth grade teacher, Mr. Gervitz told Ms. Johnson that he could always single out the kids in his class that belong to Zion Missionary Baptist Church because they were always enthusiastic, disciplined, outgoing, and well-behaved. He further commented that the children's choir and youth ministries at Zion must be dynamic to help produce young people like my daughter and the other youth he experienced coming from Zion." Mrs. Johnson's daughter Chareice is now pursuing her Doctorate Degree in Psychology, and she attributes a lot of her daughter's success to the spiritual leadership of Rev. Dr. Wade Jr., Mrs. Wade, and the entire Zion Missionary Baptist Church.

I was called by the Lord to serve Him. Even in retirement, I strive to show the same diligence and dedication to doing God's will. In this healthy transition, the way in which I serve God may differ, but I am humbled to know that I still have an impact. Rev. Douglas C. Sloss, Senior Pastor of First Baptist Church in East Chicago, Indiana said, "Thanks to the wisdom and leadership of Dr. Wade, Jr. the revival to revitalize the Twin City

Pastor Wade continues to meet with the minister's alliance and has taken many of the younger pastors under his wing passing on the wisdom and experiences that he has encountered through the years.

Ministerial Alliance in East Chicago was a great success. The mayor and most of the city officials were in attendance, but more importantly, the Lord was there. God moved in a mighty way, lives were changed and souls were saved. Pastor Wade continues to meet with the minister's alliance and has taken many of the younger pastors under his wing passing on the wisdom and experiences that he has encountered through the years. We are so blessed in that just because he retired from the pastorate, he did not retire from ministry. He has faithfully continued helping those pastors that are coming behind him. I thank God for the gift of Rev. Dr. Wade, Jr. in my life."

My cousin Alonzo Temple, a retired science teacher once told me that the Law of Physics states "a body at rest remains at rest, while a body in motion remains in motion unless acted upon by some outside force." The mindset is that when you retire and do nothing, your body remains at rest and you accomplish very little or nothing at all. On the other hand, when you do something during retirement your body remains in motion, and you can accomplish great things with the Lord's help. Continuing to serve God even after retirement is a truly blessed and healthy transition.

The Charge Continues in Retirement

"I press toward the mark for the prize of the
high calling of God in Christ Jesus,"
(Philippians 3:14).

In retirement we must be convinced that God is not going to waste our time. If we are where God wants us to be in ministry, we must ask him to fulfill his purpose in us while there. God knows who we are and will accomplish his will in our lives, but only when we have been faithful to the one that has been given authority over us. God elevates the faithful even in retirement. The famed Oscar is awarded to supporting actors as well. We must concentrate on being faithful and not famous. "Faithfulness is forever." As pastors in retirement, we are to help people see what faithfulness really means.

There is a story of an old man who carried a little can of oil everywhere he went. If he passed through a door that squeaked he poured a little oil on the hinges. If a gate was hard to open he oiled the latch. What he did was as he passed through life he made it easier for those who came after him. As I went through over 50 years of pastoral ministry, I experienced squeaky hinges and difficult latches, and I had some difficult doors to open. It was in those days that I prayed that God would use me to make it easier for the next pastor and church. So, everywhere I went I put some Spiritual Oil on things to make it easier for the next pastor and church body.

In retirement when God has officially closed the door of winter, He will open the door of spring. There is a secular metaphor called "Old Man Winter," which is suggestive of waning energy and productivity. When your energy and productivity are waning, instead of slowing down in productivity seek a new season when God opens the doorway and the entrance of spring. When the new season arrives restoration will come. Model a Reproductive Ministry. We can make a difference when we have a clear view and consciousness of the mission and mandate of Jesus who said in Matthew 28: 19-20, *"Go ye therefore, and teach all nations, baptizing them in the name of the Father, and of the Son, and of the Holy Ghost: Teaching them to observe all things whatsoever I have commanded you: and, lo, I am with you always, even unto the end of the world. Amen,"* and enhanced with compassion in order to be audible.

Learn to super-size your life. In retirement you still have some unfinished business. The question you must ask now is what is my highest calling? When you ask this question God will speak and He will speak through your heart.

In retirement you will never have a gray day when you adopt the spirit of Michael Applegate in his book *Raising a Brand New Bar*. Applegate said, "Create an attitude of appreciation. You have to re-motivate your mind, your thoughts and your attitude by developing an attitude of appreciation. Start each day by praying, smiling and thanking God for the opportunity to make your mark on the world. Be the role model for happiness, confidence, gratitude, and humility. Be the positive one, the morale booster and the light in every room you enter."

There is an old Chinese proverb that says, "When the winds of change come, some build walls, others build windmills." It is better to be flexible like the windmill than to be stubborn like the walls. When retirement time comes, leave the church better when you leave than when you came. You are not leaving a job; you are entering another season of ministry. Retirement does not mean 'the end," but it is instead "the beginning" of your new season. Pray, and allow God to direct you in your retirement.

Nicholas Smith, a young man who serves as the percussionist at Zion Missionary Baptist Church blessed me with his personal feelings about my retirement. Nicholas said, "As a young adult member of Zion Missionary Baptist Church, this transition symbolically paints the picture of a relay race in my mind. In a relay race, where one runner finishes his or her portion of the race, the next person starts. In other words, where one person's task ends, another one begins. The baton gets passed not because the runner is unable to finish the race by him or herself, but because his or her assignment has been completed. And if he or she holds on to the baton beyond the assigned length of time, the whole team will be disqualified.

I believe that many churches, businesses and organizations in general would be much better off if people realize when it is time for the baton to be passed. I am a young man now; however, if I keep living I'll have a baton to pass on to someone. And in Pastor Wade passing the mantle to Pastor Thompson, it serves as a model on how to pass the baton with God-ordained dignity."

We are not just pastors, but we are followers of Jesus Christ. When we realize that we are followers of Jesus Christ, then it will not be the size of the crowd, but the level of our commitment.   Psalms 92:12-15, *"The righteous shall flourish like the palm tree: he shall grow like a cedar in Lebanon. (13), Those that be planted in the house of the Lord shall flourish in the courts of our God. (14), They shall still bring forth fruit in old age; they shall be fat and flourishing; (15), To shew that the Lord is upright: he is my rock, and there is no unrighteousness in him."* Proverbs 20:13: *"Love not sleep, lest thou come to poverty; open thine eyes, and thou shalt be satisfied with bread."*

God's expectation for us in kingdom building does not change because we retire. We must continue to do as Apostle Paul declares in Philippians 3:14, when he said, *"I press toward the mark for the prize of the high calling of God in Christ Jesus"*

www.ingramcontent.com/pod-product-compliance
Lightning Source LLC
LaVergne TN
LVHW021500080426

835509LV00018B/2353